The Biblical Doctrine of Man

The Biblical Doctrine of Man

Gordon H. Clark

The Trinity Foundation
Jefferson, Maryland

©1984 The Trinity Foundation
Post Office Box 700
Jefferson, Maryland 21755

Second edition ©1992
The Trinity Foundation
ISBN: 0-940931-91-5

Contents

Books by Gordon H. Clark

Readings in Ethics (1931)
Selections from Hellenistic Philosophy (1940)
A History of Philosophy (coauthor, 1941)
A Christian Philosophy of Education (1946, 1988)
A Christian View of Men and Things (1952, 1991)
What Presbyterians Believe (1956)[1]
Thales to Dewey (1957, 1989)
Dewey (1960)
Religion, Reason and Revelation (1961, 1986)
William James (1963)
Karl Barth's Theological Method (1963)
The Philosophy of Science and Belief in God (1964, 1987)
What Do Presbyterians Believe? (1965, 1985)
Peter Speaks Today (1967)[2]
The Philosophy of Gordon H. Clark (1968)
Biblical Predestination (1969)[3]
Historiography: Secular and Religious (1971)
II Peter (1972)[2]
The Johannine Logos (1972, 1989)
Three Types of Religious Philosophy (1973, 1989)
First Corinthians (1975, 1991)
Colossians (1979, 1989)
Predestination in the Old Testament (1979)[3]
I and II Peter (1980)
Language and Theology (1980)
First John (1980)
God's Hammer: The Bible and Its Critics (1982, 1987)
Behaviorism and Christianity (1982)
Faith and Saving Faith (1983, 1990)
In Defense of Theology (1984)
The Pastoral Epistles (1984)
The Biblical Doctrine of Man (1984, 1992)
The Trinity (1985, 1990)
Logic (1985, 1988)
Ephesians (1985)
Clark Speaks From the Grave (1986)
Logical Criticisms of Textual Criticism (1986)
First and Second Thessalonians (1986)
Predestination (1987)
The Atonement (1987)
The Incarnation (1988)
Today's Evangelism: Counterfeit or Genuine? (1990)

[1] Revised in 1965 as *What Do Presbyterians Believe?*
[2] Combined in 1980 as *I & II Peter.*
[3] Combined in 1987 as *Predestination.*

Foreword

In twentieth century America there are many views of man. One of the most popular is the naturalist view. The naturalist view is that man is the result of an accidental collocation of atoms: Man's "number came up in the Monte Carlo games" is the way one humanist, Jacques Monod, put it.

This is in stark contrast to the Biblical view, expressed by David in the eighth Psalm:

What is man that you are mindful of him,
And the son of man that you visit him?
For you have made him a little lower than the angels,
And you have crowned him with glory and honor.
You have made him to have dominion over the works of
  your hands;
You have put all things under his feet.

This view of man, once very influential in America and throughout the world, has been subject to the prolonged attack of militant secularists. According to the naturalist view of man, God is not mindful of man, for there is no God. Even were God to exist, he would not, or could not, be conscious of man. Nor has God intervened in human history at any time. And far from being a little lower than the angels (the Hebrew actually has *Elohim,* God) man is, perhaps, a little greater than the amino acids from which he effervesced. Certainly such a position is not one of glory and honor, and man has no right to lord it over the rest of the earth; rather, he must preserve the earth. Nothing ought to be under man's feet; that is the worst form of speciesism.

The naturalist view denies every proposition that David wrote. That view has found its most eloquent expression in the words of the British mathematician and philosopher Bertrand Russell:

> That man is the product of causes that had no prevision of the end they were achieving; that his origin, his growth, his hopes and fears, his loves and his beliefs, are but the outcome of accidental collocations of atoms; that no fire, no heroism, no intensity of thought and feeling can preserve an individual life beyond the grave, that all the labors of the ages, all the devotion, all the inspiration, all the noonday brightness of human genius are destined to extinction in the vast death of the solar system, and the whole temple of Man's achievement must inevitably be buried beneath the debris of a universe in ruins—all these things, if not quite beyond dispute, are yet so nearly certain, that no philosophy which rejects them can hope to stand. Only within the scaffolding of these truths, only on the firm foundation of unyielding despair, can the soul's habitation henceforth be safely built. . . .
>
> Brief and powerless is Man's life; on him and all his race the slow, sure doom falls pitiless and dark.

Blind to good and evil, reckless of destruction, omnipotent matter rolls on its relentless way; for Man, condemned today to lose his dearest, tomorrow himself to pass through the gate of darkness, it remains only to cherish, ere yet the blow falls, the lofty thoughts that ennoble his little day. . . . proudly defiant of the irresistible forces that tolerate, for a moment, his knowledge and his condemnation, to sustain alone, a weary but unyielding Atlas, the world that his own ideals have fashioned despite the trampling march of unconscious power.

It is no accident that both Monod and Russell began by denying God and end by advocating the creation of a totalitarian world government. Monod called for "some form of world authority" to manage a "stable-state society." Russell advocated "the creation of a single world-wide authority, possessing a monopoly of all the more serious weapons. . . . the vital point is the placing of irresistible force in the hands of the central authority. . . . The central Government may be democratic or totalitarian; it may owe its origin to consent or to conquest. . . . I do not believe that the human race has sufficient statesmanship or capacity for mutual forbearance to establish a world Government on a basis of consent alone. That is why I think that an element of force will be needed in its establishment and in its preservation through the early years of its existence. . . . Modern man is master of his fate."

Those who attack God attack his image, man. They have no scruples about herding and slaughtering men like animals. Despite what Russell said, modern man is not the master of his fate. What Russell's phrase actually means is that some men are masters of the fates of other men. The totalitarianism of the humanists is a logical and inexorable consequence of their humanism.

The Biblical Doctrine of Man is a most necessary book, least of all for political reasons. There are spiritual as well as political totalitarians at work in the world, and the doctrines they teach, if believed, will lead one to hell, not merely to a concentration camp. Many of their opinions have the appearance of piety, just as the Devil himself sometimes appears as an angel of light.

The spiritual totalitarians teach that man's mind is incapable of knowing God: Barth and Kierkegaard maintain that man must understand and believe contradictions about God, for God is totally different from man. Still others teach that human language is incapable of expressing divine truth. And all would have us believe that the Bible itself contains irreconcilable contradictions. These views, which implicitly deny that man is the likeness of God, subvert all Christianity, for Christianity asserts that man can know God, that the Bible is both man's words and God's words, and that it contains no error. The truth, as Christ said, shall make us free. We sometimes forget that he first said, You shall know the truth.

The proper view of man is second in importance only to the proper view of God. If either is misunderstood or rejected, the consequences for this life are death and tyranny; the consequences for the next life are infinitely worse: never-ending hell.

John Robbins
December 1991

In 1895 John Laidlaw, Professor of Theology in New College, Edinburgh, published his revised edition of *The Bible Doctrine of Man.* It is a masterpiece, and every theological student should study it with great care. The present attempt cannot equal it; but perhaps some references to twentieth century developments, and inevitably from another person's perspective, may justify this attempt. What unfortunately justifies this attempt to a greater degree is the disturbing fact that so few contemporary students have read its illustrious predecessor.

The main topics discussed here are the creation of man, the nature of man as given in creation, the propagation of the soul to Adam's descendants, the religious relation of Adam as the first man to his posterity, and the effects of sin, noetic and otherwise. The subject matter is somewhat more complicated than these section headings may suggest.

1. Creation and Evolution

God created man, men, the human race as he also created the solar system and the sand of the sea. It hardly needs mention that the Bible teaches a theistic philosophy. But though equally created, man differs from the sea and the solar system in nature and importance. The physical universe is but a backdrop or stage setting for the Divine Comedy in which man is the main actor. In the largest sense God is the main actor, as well as the author. But among created things, when history is taken as the drama of redemption, man plays the title role. Some people, called scientists, legitimately study the stage setting with its lighting arrangements, but "the play's the thing."

Now first, the Bible definitely asserts that man was created.

Genesis 1:27   So God created man in his own image, in the image of God created he him; male and female, created he them.

Genesis 2:21-23   and the Lord caused a deep sleep to fall upon Adam, and he took one of his ribs, and . . . made he a woman . . . and Adam said, This is now bone of my bones . . . She shall be called woman.

Acts 17:26   God . . . hath made of one blood all nations of men.

1

Adam was created a full grown adult. Eve was miraculously taken from his side. And the human race descended from this pair.

Brief as the above statement is, it is enough to show that the Bible assigns the origin of man to God's command. But not everyone believes the Bible. From reports in the public media one easily gets the impression that only a small and ignorant minority of the population believes the Bible. The present study aims to explain the Biblical position. But to a degree it must also defend that position against the assaults of its adversaries. But only to a degree, for the problems involved extend to the profoundest depths of philosophy where many a gem of purest ray serene is borne to waste its fragrance on the desert air.

Throughout the twentieth century the most vigorous attack on the divine creation of man has been the theory of evolution. In the United States its exponents have obtained governmental compulsion of its teaching and governmental prohibition of the theistic view. Perhaps this is an indication of the intellectual weakness of the evolutionary theory. Scholars used to insist on freedom of thought and expression. Today the organized educators use legal force to ban the view they dislike. This method of legal repression may be subconsciously supported by the suspicion that scientific theories are tentative only. In physics the Newtonian synthesis has been abandoned. One can say that in biology Darwinianism is not universally accepted; and what new theories century twenty-one will see, no one can guess. The evolutionists must rely on political restraint.

There are some interesting side-lights in this battle for religious liberty and scholarly freedom. Although there are pictorial diagrams of the descent of man, with the Piltdown man erased, the evolutionists have not produced a similar botanical genealogy, though this should precede zoology. Then too, there is a sociological aberration. Religious liberals react strongly against anything, no matter how innocent, that remotely resembles what they call racism. The mainstay of their religion is the Fatherhood of God and the Brotherhood of Man. But it is the Biblical doctrine of creation that makes all men natural brothers. This is something that evolution cannot do. Evolution allows men to have evolved in several places at several times. Thus the liberals' science conflicts with their religion. Nor can their religion be commended for making Stalin and Hitler the spiritual brothers of the apostle Paul.

A further word on the Piltdown Man will show how the theory of evolution corrupts the scientific process. Someone in England planted a hoax where he knew that excavations would soon be made. He used chemicals to age the tooth of an ape and buried it. When the excavators found it, the scientist-cartoonists blew it up with jaws, hair, legs, torso, and called it the Piltdown Man. Museums displayed him to overawed visitors. There were, however, a few, a very few, reputable scientists who were cautious and skeptical. But so great was their submission to the theory of evolution that they finally capitulated to the majority opinion. It was almost half a century later that the dishonesty of the perpetrator and the uninhibited imagination of the reconstructors were discovered. During all that time the Piltdown Man was a standard item of evolutionary proof in college zoology courses.

That the Bible has a theistic view widely different from contemporary biology is already clear in the few verses quoted above. They teach that the human race is one race descended from precisely two human beings. But the Bible's most conspicuous denial of evolution is the second citation, Genesis 2:21, on the creation or formation of woman. It is not clear whether evolution must hold that the first human being was a male or female; and it would be stretching credulity to suppose that a pair always evolved at the same time and place. But Eve was no evolutionary product. She did not appear in the usual way. So-called natural law does not cover her case. Therefore the usual forms of evolution, even with occasional theistic modifications, cannot be harmonized with Christianity, for Christianity teaches creation.

In this scientific debate one should press upon the biologists and the federal courts what most physics professors know so well: namely, that science is not fixed but tentative. There used to be a universal ether by which light waves were propagated. But a good ninety years ago that ether evaporated. The result was that light became and remains today self-contradictory "wavicles." Atomism exploded, theoretically in 1905, and visibly in World War II. The Newtonian law of gravitation, supposedly describing the motion of all bodies and accounting for the distribution of the planets and stars, held sway for two centuries. But now not one of the Newtonian laws remains. Even the first law of straight line motion is gone, for there is no scientific method for determining a straight line. Subsidiary laws, such as the theory of heat, had changed earlier. But the evolutionists, particularly those in Education, blindly believe that their view is immutably true.

Because of the present work of the Institute of Creation Research, and the court cases concerning the legal imposition of one particular view upon school children, many Christians are beginning to understand that not only legal action but also scientific study is a necessary concern. A few realize that Christians should consider physics as well as zoology and geology. But many see no point in studying philosophy. Yet the nature of man is subject for both psychology and philosophy. The early Christian fathers who formulated our basic doctrines adopted, modified, or denied the views of Plato,

Chrysippus, and Philo. In modern times various orthodox theologians utilize the views of Descartes, Locke, or Kant, sometimes without realizing what they are doing. The result has usually been some distortion, great or small, of both the Bible and the philosopher. The secular scientist says that theology hinders science; but often Christians have hindered theology by imposing current scientific theories on the Bible. The best way to avoid this error is to know the several non-christian systems. Only then can one be confident that foreign theories have not contaminated theology. Hence zoology, physics, and philosophy too demand discussion in a study of the Bible.

2. The Image of God

Instead of assigning to man a subhuman ancestry, the Bible teaches that man was created in the image of God. On one occasion, in a philosophy class, a girl dressed in the synthetic poverty of dirty blue jeans, popular in the 1960's, objected to a Christian expression in the lecture and replied, "But I am only an animal." She was in truth a human being, however poor a specimen. The Bible makes an immense distinction between man and animals. Animals are interesting, sometimes clever, and often beautiful. One of the most handsome specimens I ever saw was an enormous skunk. About three times the size of ordinary skunks, he would have been a prize for any skunk basketball or football team. I was tempted to make his acquaintance, but thought better of it. After a moment or two we bowed to each other and went our opposite ways. Likewise, who is not intrigued by a road runner, and who fails to admire a lion or jaguar? In the zoo, of course.

In order to describe the nature of the image one can

immediately assert the principle that any interpretation which identifies the image with some characteristics not found in God must be incorrect. For example, the image cannot be man's body. If anyone says that the upright position of the human body, in contrast with fourfooted beasts and creeping things, allows it to be the image, the reply is not merely that birds have two legs, but rather that Genesis makes no reference to a physical image. A more important reason for denying that man's body is the image is the fact that God is not and has not a body.

One can at the same time see a more notable distinction between the creation of animals and the creation of man. In Genesis 1:11 we read, "Let the earth bring forth grass;" a few verses further on, "God said, Let the waters bring forth abundantly." Verse 24 adds, "Let the earth bring forth cattle and every creeping thing and beasts." But Genesis 1:26, 27 quote God as saying, "Let us make man in our image;" and then continue, "So God created man in his own image." Because the earth brings forth cattle, while God says "Let us," the wording suggests a more direct relationship between God and man than between God and the animals. Animals are indeed beautiful and interesting and useful; but man is superior. How?

Although the two verses just quoted do not explain exactly how, the context implies more than one might guess at first reading. To be sure, Genesis says that God gave man dominion over the animals; but it is more important to know by what endowment such a dominion can be exercised. We might guess by noting that although the Baltimore oriole builds a beautiful nest, oriole architecture has not changed in centuries. One can also note that animals cannot do geometry nor even write narrative. These missing activities depend on a rationality that animals lack. We call them brute species. Man has a mind.

Let us therefore examine with greater care how much Genesis actually implies. More important than the dominion itself is the fact that God explained this dominion to Adam. That is to say, God spoke to Adam and Adam understood what God told him. To understand meaningful speech requires more intelligence than it does to manage animals.

Then too, God's instructions to Adam were not limited to agriculture and husbandry. He gave Adam some religious instructions also. Genesis 2:16, 17 record certain commands that God imposed on Adam. In particular God commanded Adam not to eat the fruit of a certain tree, and he warned him that "in the day thou eatest thereof thou shalt surely die." Here we have a stated penalty for disobedience. How did Adam know what death was? For what matter how did Adam know that he was obligated to obey? These are matters of the knowledge of morality, and Adam understood. If we must go to the New Testament to see it more clearly, I Timothy 2:14 tells us that though Eve was deceived, Adam was not deceived. Clearly Adam understood.

But there is another point that precedes and is requisite to Adam's disobedience. In addition to understanding his dominion over the animals, and in addition to his, perhaps incomplete, understanding of the creation of Eve, as stated in Genesis 1:23, 24, Adam also recognized his friendly and happy relationship with God. This is partly shown in the fact that neither Adam nor Eve was ashamed of being naked. It is better shown in the recorded conversation between God and Adam. God had endowed Adam with the ability to speak, not only to speak to Eve, but to speak to God and worship him. The whole account in the first chapter depicts an unspoiled relationship. This relationship, which one may call a religious relationship, continues in a negative fashion after Adam sinned. The conversation is recorded in Gensis 3:18-19. When Adam heard the voice of the Lord God, he and his wife hid themselves, and God said, "Where art thou?" Adam replied, "I was afraid." And so the account proceeds. The important point is that God and Adam talked to each other and Adam understood. Animals do not understand, are not subject to moral commands, cannot sin, and hold no religious services.

In describing the image of God as it was before the fall, it is almost impossible to exclude a reference to man's later condition. Since man is himself the image, as the following paragraph will explain, the image must in some way or other be a permanent characteristic of personality. Original righteousness reveals a capacity of man's nature for restoration after sin. Had Adam never been either moral or intelligent before the fall, no one could assert the possibility of his later becoming so. But since he was so before the fall, the impossibility of a restoration is ruled out.

If Adam's condition in Eden had not been that of original righteousness, but only a neutral condition, neither good nor bad, there would be little hope of a more blessed future. Pelagians and Romanists hold that man was originally neutral. God created him without a moral character. He had only a capacity to become good or bad. This assumes that moral character is a product of volition, instead of volition's being controlled by the character. But God's pronouncement that the creation was good, and that the creation of man was very good, shows that Adam's original nature was not an equilibrium. And the argument shows how one doctrine affects another so that theology is not an aggregate of propositions, but a system.

Proceeding further into the Old Testament one finds that Job 32:8 repeats the idea of intellect or understanding. It says, "The inspiration of the Almighty giveth them [men] understanding." Isaiah 42:5 may be less clear, yet it contains the same idea: "He giveth breath unto the people . . . and spirit to them that walk [on earth]." When we come to the New Testament remarkable additions are found. The image of God is not something man has, somewhere inside of him, or somewhere on the surface, as if God had first created man and then stamped him with a signet ring. No, the image is not something man *has*, man *is* the image. First Corinthians 11:7 pointedly says, "He [man] is the image and glory of God."

So much for exegesis for the moment. There are other complications, perhaps more philosophical than some would prefer, which nevertheless must be fitted into the material from Genesis. Some contemporary theologians, on the whole quite orthodox, insist that man is a unity, not a duality; hence they conclude that he is not his soul, but the combination of soul and body.

Before discussing such a view, one should realize that the New Testament terminology, though a development from the Old, is not precisely the same. Genesis explicitly describes the soul as the combination of earthly clay and divine breath, and calls man a living soul. The language in the preceding paragraph takes soul to be something quite distinct from the body, and this in general is the New Testament usage. While the Old Testament often uses soul and spirit synonymously, the New Testament, especially when the adjectival forms of the word occur, imposes on them a moral distinction. Soulish carries an evil connotation (compare I Corinthians 2:14, 15:44, Jude 19). On the other hand, spiritual no longer denotes the human spirit, but the influence of the Holy Ghost (compare I Corinthians 2:11-16 and 15:42-47; Colossians 1:9, I Peter 2:5).

With this Scriptural background in mind, one may return to the question, not whether man is a unity, but what sort of unity man is. A parallel case should help. Salt is a sort of unity too, being the chemical combination of sodium and chlorine.

So also the compound man is not the soul. Here of course the word *soul* does not reproduce the usage of *nephesh* in Genesis 2:7. It is a New Testament usage and is the common usage of our present century. Now, to show that man himself is not the combination, but is precisely the soul, mind, or spirit, one may appeal to II Corinthians 12:2, which says that on one occasion Paul did not know whether or not he was in the body or out of the body. Quite obviously the *he* cannot be the body, for he, Paul, could be either in the body or out of it. And if man *is* the soul, we have a more perfect unity than a chemical compound of sodium and chlorine. One may also quote II Corinthians 5:1, "For we know that if our earthly home of the tabernacle be destroyed, we have a building of God, a house not made with hands, eternal in the heavens." Similarly Philippians 1:21 ff. says, "For to me to live is Christ and to die is gain . . . for I am faced with two choices, having the desire to depart and be with Christ, for this is far better. . . ." Both of these verses show that the person can exist apart from the body. The body is not the person; it is a place in which the soul dwells. The home eternal in the heavens is not the soul, for our souls are not eternal. By God's grace they are everlasting, but eternality would be a denial of their creation. What Paul is saying is that if the soul's present residence is to be destroyed, we need not worry because in our Father's house there are many mansions, and Christ has ascended to prepare them for the arrival of our souls. Or to change the figure, the present body, as Augustine said, is an instrument which the soul uses. It is the latter that is the image and the person.

Though the two verses just quoted come from Paul, Peter teaches the same doctrine when he says that he will shortly put off this earthly tabernacle. The body had been his house or tent. He himself would soon move to more elaborate quarters.

This dispenses with the notion that the body is a part of

the image. The image is the soul. Indeed the soul is more than an image. Of all the passages quoted, I Corinthians 11:7, previously used to show that man is the image, remains the strongest of all, for it adds an astounding phrase. It says that man is not only the image of God, but also that man is the glory of God. Only the authority of direct revelation permits this assertion. Hodge in his commentary on I Corinthians offers an explanation of this additional designation, but it is sufficient here simply to recognize how emphatic it is.

This view of man seems to maintain the unity of the person better than its rivals; it seems to be more consistent and logical; and with all the Scriptural support indicated it seems impossible to find a view that is more Biblical. Since the doctrine is so important relative to soteriology, it may be interesting, if not essential, to see how the early church began to study the subject.

3. Some Earlier Views

The idea that God created man in his own image is so clearly stated in Genesis that the early church fathers could not miss it. It is also such an amazing idea that they could not refrain from discussing it. Some of the first attempts were, naturally, less than intelligible. For example, Gregory of Nyssa expatiates in flowery metaphors conveying awe of the subject, but which lack any explanatory clarity. Well, perhaps there is one clear point: The image has something to do with human intelligence. This is at least better than Justin Martyr's identification of it with the bodily form. Augustine took the image to be the knowledge of the truth and he took the likeness to be the love of virtue. In his *Summa Theologica* (Q. 93, Art. 9) after stating some views to be rejected, Thomas Aquinas in his usual form writes, "*On the contrary,* Augustine says, 'Some consider that these two were mentioned not without reason, namely image and likeness, since if they meant the same, one would have sufficed.' " This attempt to distinguish rather than to identify image and likeness was not one of Augustine's happiest tentatives. If the Bible were written in the technical language of Aristotle's *Metaphysics,* one could well imagine that the two words bore different meanings. But in literary language such as the Bible uses, two such words can be synonymously used for the sake of emphasis. The Psalms are replete with this device: "I *cried* unto Thee, O Lord, and unto the Lord I made my *supplication;*" and "Blessed is he whose *transgression* is *forgiven,* and whose *sin* is *covered,*" where there are two pairs of synonyms; and "Thy word is a *lamp* unto my feet and a *light* unto my path." There are many such.

Even so, it is not fatal to the doctrines of grace if a distinction, without faulty additions, is made between image and likeness. Since the New Testament refers to knowledge and righteousness, we could call the one the image and the other the likeness. Such a speculation, however, is rather fanciful and futile. One must therefore consider what distinction the Roman church imposed on the terms and how it fitted into a distortion of Biblical truth.

In support of the distinction Thomas had already (Q. 93, Art. 1) argued that where an image exists, there must be a likeness; but a likeness does not necessarily mean an image. Now, the Roman church developed this, which so far is innocuous, into something that contradicts important parts of the Biblical message. Their present view is that the image itself is rationality, created because, when, and as man was created. But after man was created, God gave him an extra gift, a *donum superadditum,* the likeness, defined as original righteousness. Man therefore was not strictly created righteous. Adam was at first morally neutral. Perhaps he was not even neutral. Bellarmin speaks of the original Adam, composed of body and soul, as disordered and diseased, afflicted with a *morbus* or languor that needed a remedy. Yet Bellarmin does not quite say that this *morbus* is a sin; it is rather something unfortunate and less than ideal. To remedy this defect God gave the additional gift of righteousness. Adam's fall then resulted in the loss of original righteousness; but he fell only to the neutral moral level on which he was created. In this state, because of his free will, he is able, at least in some low degree, to please God.

Obviously this view has soteriological implications. Even though the neutral state was soon defaced by voluntary sins, man without saving grace could still obey God's commands upon occasion. After regeneration a man could do even more than God requires. This then becomes the foundation of the Roman Catholic doctrine of the treasury of the saints. If a particular man does not himself earn a sufficient number of merits, the Pope can transfer from the saints' accounts as many more merits as are necessary for his entrance into heaven. One horrendous implication of all this is that although Christ's death remains necessary to salvation, it is not sufficient. Human merit is indispensable.

However logically implicated this soteriology is, the present study should not stray too far from the image itself. Above it was said that an assertion of a distinction between image and likeness, by itself, is not fatal. But it is not Biblical either. Scripture makes no distinction between image and likeness. Not only does the New Testament make nothing of such a distinction; even in Genesis the two words are used interchangeably. Genesis 1:27 uses the word *image* alone, and Genesis 5:1 uses *likeness* alone, though in each case the whole is intended. The likeness therefore is not an extra gadget attached to man after his creation, not a *donum superadditum,* like a suit of clothes that he could take off. It is rather the unitary person.

4. The Definition

This short account of earlier views has somewhat trespassed on the territory of the nature of the image. That knowledge, and possibly righteousness, have commonly been associated with man's original endowment is a point no reader above third grade can have missed. The majority of devout evangelical Christians would probably stress righteousness, and if the subject were soteriology that would be proper. But during the second half of the twentieth century a rather pointed debate has centered on the factor of knowledge. As an important development in apologetics it has become a bit technical. Even so, the debaters try to base their views on Scripture. Let us begin with one important passage.

Since the verses in Genesis imply more than they state, the first verse to be quoted, and for the purpose of showing that Scripture defines the image as knowledge and righteousness, is Colossians 3:10. The definition is derived by noting that the new man is such because God has renewed him after the image in which he was originally created. Ephesians 4:24 mentions righteousness, but Colossians has knowledge only. Its previous context speaks of "the old man with deeds." Then comes a contrast with "the new man." In what consists the renewal that makes the old man the new man? The verse says, He is renewed "to knowledge." He is renewed to knowledge according to the image of the Creator. That is to say, the image of God, in which image man was created, is knowledge. Of course this does not mean that Adam was omniscient; yet he had some knowledge, and this is not said of the animals. Since this knowledge comes by the act of breathing into Adam the spirit of life, the knowledge must be considered, not as the result of observation, since Adam had not yet observed anything at all, but as the apriori or the innate equipment for learning.

If it be suggested that angels also have rational knowledge, they too must have been created in God's image and therefore man is not the only image of God. This is plausible since the Psalms say that man was created a little lower than the angels. But it does not militate against man's being the image of God. And further, while the Bible distinctly asserts the image in man, it does not make this assertion of angels. The creation of angels is left in obscurity, and so we too must leave it there.

A study of the nature of man can become complex, cannot avoid becoming complex. But because sin is a disturbing factor, it is easier to study man in his original state of innocency. Modern psychology and secular philosophy face extreme difficulties. Six hundred years after Socrates said, "Know thyself," Plotinus wrote fifty-four tractates on the problem. Here we reject that well known bad advice, "Seek not the face of God to scan, the proper study of mankind is man." Contrary to this advice we do indeed seek the face of God to scan, and for the very reason that one of the proper studies of mankind is man. Without a revelation from God who made man, it is doubtful that we could learn much about him at all. Even with the aid of a divine revelation the subject is still difficult.

The Bible asks the question, "What is man?" Can we answer what a person is? Do you know yourself? The Bible also says, "The heart of man is desperately wicked: who can know it?" Can we know the heart or nature of man before he became desperately wicked? Is man what he thinks? Or is he Immanuel Kant's "transcendental unity of apperception"? Hume described him as a group of sensations. This would make him not much superior to the animals, for many animals have sharper sensations than man has. But animals cannot think. At least they cannot do geometry, and geometry is just about the best example of thinking that one can think of. Man then is a rational being, like God, while animals, bless their little gizzards, are not.

But let us get back to the Scripture. There were two verses that connected knowledge and righteousness. Such a brief statement requires further explanation. We need additional information because a correct view of the original nature of man must underlie, not only an understanding of sin and the fall, but also the Biblical view of death, the intermediate state, the resurrection, and our final beatitude. To repeat: Theology is systematic: All its parts interpenetrate each other.

Genesis clearly distinguishes man from animals. Every book in the Bible describes sinful man as thinking, often thinking incorrectly, but sometimes thinking correctly. We must more closely examine Adam as he was before the fall; but to provide a background, without which one's view would be too restricted, some other parts of Scripture will be more or less haphazardly introduced.

The image must be reason because God is truth, and fellowship with him—a most important purpose in creation—requires thinking and understanding. Without reason man would doubtless glorify God as do the stars, stones, and animals; but he could not enjoy him forever. Even if in God's providence animals survive death and adorn the heavenly realm, they cannot have what the Scripture calls eternal life because eternal life consists in knowing the only true God, and knowledge is an exercise of the mind or reason. Without reason there can be no morality or righteousness: These too require thought. Lacking these, animals are neither righteous nor sinful.

The identification of the image with reason explains or is supported by a puzzling remark in John 1:9: "It was the true light that lighteth every man that cometh into the world." How can Christ, in whom is the life that is the light of men, be the light of every man, when Scripture teaches that some are lost in eternal darkness? The puzzle arises from interpreting light in exclusively redemptive terms.

The first chapter of John is not soteriological only. Obviously there are references to salvation in verses 7, 8, 12, and 13. It is not surprising that some Christians understood verse nine also in a soteriological sense. But it is not true that all men are saved; hence if Christ lightens every man, this enlightening cannot be soteriological. This is not the only non-soteriological verse in the chapter. The opening verses treat of creation and the relation of the Logos to God. If the enlightening is not soteriological, it could be epistemological. Then since responsibility depends on knowledge, the responsibility of the unregenerate is adequately founded.

In order to avoid this interpretation and to retain the idea of salvation here, one exegete suggests that the Light shines on all but does not penetrate all. He might even have quoted earlier verses that the light shines in darkness and the darkness did not grasp or understand it. But the later verse does not speak of darkness in the abstract; it speaks of all men. Can it now be said that the light lights all men without enlightening them?

The verb occurs about eleven times in the New Testament. First, Luke 11:36. The passage begins with literal light (though artificial) by which people are enabled to see in an otherwise dark room. It then speaks of the whole body's being full of light. There is no hint that the people do not see the light. Quite the reverse; and the last phrase asserts that the person receives the light.

I Corinthians 4:5 might be taken as an example of "casting light upon," without enlightening any mind. This is irrelevant, however, for the objects on which the light shines are not human beings but the hidden things of darkness. Even so, the persons twice obliquely alluded to, seem to achieve perception thereby.

Ephesians 1:18, "The eyes of your hearts being enlightened to know . . ." is a strong confirmation of the interpretation now being given to John 1:9. Ephesians 3:9 is also similar. That the light gives or is the knowledge cannot be denied.

When II Timothy 1:10 says that Christ "brought life and immortality to light," it must mean the implantation of knowledge in men because this lighting or enlightening was accompanied by the preaching of the gospel. The passage is indeed soteric, but the lighting is subjective or individual.

Subjective enlightenment is also found in Hebrews 6:4 and 10:32.

Revelation 18:1 could well be a lighting effect on objects without any change in the mind of a human being. Revelation 21:23 could be the same, though the next verse says that human beings took advantage of the light.

It is not to be denied that most of these references are soteric. John 1:9 cannot be soteric because it refers to all men. But this is far from showing that the light hits them in a merely external way, as it might shine on a rock or tree. The conclusion therefore is that creative light gives every man an innate knowledge sufficient to make all men responsible for their evil actions. This interpretation ties in with the idea of creation in verse three. Thus the Logos or rationality of God, who created all things without a single exception, can be seen as having created man with the light of logic as his distinctive human characteristic.

5. Apriorism

During the second half of the twentieth century apologetes, most of them otherwise orthodox, have tried to develop a theism based on sensory experience. Some of them are satisfied with a Thomistic cosmological argument for the existence of God without explicitly producing a complete empirical epistemology. Others seem satisfied with even less: Sometimes called evidentialists, they have tried to prove the truth of the Bible by archaeological discoveries. One at least is chiefly interested in history. A few go some distance into epistemology, but they usually, I could even say always, ignore basic questions, such as the production of abstract ideas from memory images. Examples of these somewhat varying groups are Stuart C. Hackett in his *The Resurrection of Theism;* Gordon R. Lewis in his *Testing Christianity's Truth Claims;* and several works by John Warwick Montgomery, Clark Pinnock, and R.C. Sproul. There are differences among them, of course. Some are more explicit than others. Some are more consistent than others. But in general they are empiricists, denying apriori forms of the mind, and implicitly basing all knowledge on sensation.

This view has had a long and illustrious history. It began with Aristotle, from whom Thomas Aquinas derived his basic principles; John Locke had a slightly different version of it, which Augustus Toplady unfortunately pretty much accepted; plus John Gill, and with certain modifications, Charles Hodge and B.B. Warfield. Probably because of the latter two the Platonic or Augustinian view has been often frowned upon.

The Lutherans too, as for example Leander S. Keyser, have generally been Aristotelians. But not all. Dorner in his *A System of Christian Doctrine* (Edinburgh, 1881, Vol. II, p. 82) asserts that "the soul is never a mere *tabula rasa*, . . . there is in it a world of the unconscious. If in our knowledge there is already inherent no innate relation to what is rational and good—a relation that is an original dowry of our nature and not our own work—then knowledge of truth and goodness as such is absolutely out of the question." This is a statement worth reading a second time.

If further Lutheran documentation is desired, one will find a less explicit and no doubt a different point of view in Francis Pieper's *Christian Dogmatics* (Concordia Publishing House, 1950). In the section entitled "Man Before the Fall," he agrees that "image and likeness are synonyms," citing the verses quoted here. Though using slightly different language, he also accepts knowledge and righteousness as its components. But surely he exaggerates the extent of Adam's knowledge when he says that Adam "had such a grasp of the natural sciences as is unattainable today by even the most diligent study" (I, p. 517). Did Adam really foresee the recent upsetting discoveries about the rings of Saturn? Or the implanting of a mechanical heart in a human being? Aside from such imaginations, the basic difficulty, from the point of view of this discussion, is that Pieper seems to have no interest in the epistemological problem and therefore simply avoids it.

John Theodore Mueller, in his *Christian Dogmatics*, emulates his Lutheran predecessor. He is slightly more explicit than Pieper, and continues the exaggeration of Adam's knowledge. The difference is that Adam's whole scientific knowledge is pictured as apriori. Disturbed by evolution he wrote, "The evolutionistic view, according to which man was originally a brute, without the faculty of speech . . . is therefore antiscriptural. . . . In addition to perfect moral endowments man was blessed also with great intellectual endowments, so that he possessed . . . an intuitive knowledge of God's creatures (science) such as no scientist after the Fall has ever attained" (p. 205). Note that whereas Pieper simply assigned to Adam the same extensive knowledge, Mueller adds that this knowledge was "intuitive." If Adam's correct knowledge of the speed of light was not empirical but intuitive, the term *intuitive* seems to mean apriori. In any case no such extensive knowledge is ascribed to Adam in the Scriptural verses Mueller quotes, *viz.*, Genesis 2:19-20, 23-24. Neither writer is sufficiently clear, but the phrase "great intellectual endowment" and the word "intuitive" favor apriorism much more than they favor empiricism.

Unfortunately, however, Mueller had previously approved of the cosmological argument for the existence of God (p. 143) as Pieper also had done before him. The two authors lack consistency. Neither of them seems interested in the present problem, nor is either so clear as Dorner.

Dorner rejected the blank mind. Even some Roman Catholics, a few centuries ago, defended apriorism: Descartes, Malebranche, Pascal, and the Jansenists. But all the wit of Pascal did not save them from the Jesuits.

Now, it seems to me that even the skimpy material in Genesis is sufficient to refute empiricism with its blank mind. First, since God is a God of knowledge, eternally omniscient, how could a being, declared to be his image and likeness, be a blank mind? Even apart from the explicit statements in the New Testament, Genesis says that God commanded Adam and Eve to be fruitful and multiply. Since at that time they had no sensory experience of other people, must they not have had some innate intelligence to understand this command? Of course an empiricist might insist that they had learned the meaning from observing animals. But this assumes that a fair length of time intervened between the creation of Adam and God's imposition of the obligation. One can better suppose that God gave instructions to Adam more immediately. This is rather obviously true of Genesis 2:16, 17. The command not to eat of a given tree, since it constituted Adam's probation, surely was given only moments after the creation. Of course such a command was not apriori knowledge, but the intellectual equipment to understand it was.

There is more, too. Adam not only understood the command: He understood that it was God who gave it. Are we to suppose that he laboriously worked out the cosmological argument, including the physics that underlies it? And did he derive the concept of moral responsibility from his sensations? Though the account is brief, it seems that Adam knew he was obligated to worship God and obey him. But empiricism's cosmological argument is surpassed in its fallacies by the impossibility of deducing moral evaluations from factual premises, even should these premises be true. If an empiricist insists that the Genesis account is too brief to support such an interpretation, we can at least rely on the Pauline epistles. Genesis is not the only book in the Bible.

A subsidiary point is Cain's fear of punishment after he had murdered Abel. Evidently God had given Adam and his boys what we call the sixth commandment. They must have recognized this as a moral imperative. But is it at all possible to develop the idea of a moral imperative by watching trees grow in a garden? Note the point: The commandment itself may not have been innate, but the idea of morality must have been or the import of the commandment could not have been understood. Sensation at best might possibly give some factual information; but though this would be knowledge of what *is,* empiricism can never produce a knowledge of what *ought* to be.

Underlying all these details of both physics and morality lies the necessity of universal propositions. Not only are murder and idolatry wrong, but the laws of physics are asserted as applying universally. They are not supposed to have any exceptions. Physics is the clearer example. The law of the pendulum, to take an elementary example, is that the period of the swing is proportional to the square root of the length. The law asserts that this is true of all pendulums, all that exist now, all that have existed in the past, and all that will exist in the future. The law is a universal proposition, that is, it has no exceptions. Clearly this law cannot have been deduced from experiment or observation, for no one has observed all present pendulums, or all past pendulums, and no one has observed any future pendulums. Hence empiricism can never justify any law of physics. If, now, sensory experience cannot justify a knowledge of natural phenomena, how could it possibly be of any use in theology? The principles of theology are all universal propositions. Of course theology includes certain historical statements, such as "David was king of Israel," and this does not seem to be a universal. Actually it is, for David as the subject term is a class by himself, and all of that class is a king of Israel. But aside from propositions with individual subjects, the principles of theology, which give meaning to the historical events, are plain, ordinary universal statements. They cannot therefore be based on observation. For that matter, God cannot be observed.

In addition to the failure of empiricism due to universal propositions, there is an even more fundamental factor. Every statement, even if particular, depends on the law of contradiction. Truth and error are incompatible. If all marhoucals are rhinosaps, there cannot be a single marhoucal that is not a rhinosap. We do not have to inspect the infinite number of the latter in order to assure ourselves that none can be found.

Given the premise we do not need to examine even one. That O ab cannot be deduced from A ab is a necessity of logic. And if our minds are not so constructed, we can never distinguish truth from error. But empiricism furnishes no necessity, no universality, no *all*, no *none.*

Indeed, it furnishes no *some* either. Whether the logical form be universal or particular, the proposition must have a subject term. All dogs are vertebrates; some dogs are black. Suppose now that the subject term, dogs, had five meanings. This is not unusual for English words. Consult *Merriam Webster's Unabridged Dictionary.* Look up the words fast, curb, domestic, race, land, not to mention love, emotion, grace, religion, and virtue. Each one will have possibly four, five, and sometimes six different meanings. This frequently introduces considerable ambiguity, with the result that an argument, apparently logical, is actually fallacious. The fallacy can be avoided, sometimes with a bit of trouble, by specifying meaning one, meaning two, and meaning three. But there is a deeper problem. Suppose a given word had an infinite number of meanings. The word *fast* would then mean every word in the dictionary from the article "a" to "zyzzogetan," plus an unimaginable greater number. "Fast fast fast fast" would mean, "Today is last Tuesday" and "Washington discovered America in 1066." That is to say, a word that means everything means nothing. But this which is so obvious could not be deduced from any finite number of observations. It is a principle which must be accepted even before the term "observation" could be given any meaning at all. Therefore the use of any single word in an intelligible sentence depends on an apriori principle. No blank mind could ever discover this principle. One could phrase the principle as "a word, to mean something, must also not mean something;" or, "if a word means everything, it means nothing." Like the law of contradiction it is a way of maintaining the distinction between truth and falsehood. And this distinction is the basic element in the image of God.

6. Behaviorism

The most vigorous opponents of Platonism, Augustinianism, apriorism, intellectualism, rationalism, or whatever anyone wishes to call it, are not the Christian evidentialists. These gentlemen adopt an inconsistent amalgam of empiricism and the Biblical doctrine of the image. The logical positivists, the behaviorists, the devotees of scientism are consistent: There is no commixture of mental or spiritual ideas with corporeal concepts in their theory. Man is entirely physical, and there is no life after death.

It will be profitable to contrast the Biblical view of man as rational with behaviorism, because even many devout church members, who attend regularly, have picked up behavioristic ideas from the pervasive culture. Their minds are thus confused. Less confused are many who never attend church and who more or less definitely oppose Christianity. When the preacher or one of the devout members tries to tell them the good news, one of two things may happen. The secularist may not understand the words because of his mind-set and humanistic vocabulary. Or, and this is frequent, the secularist overwhelms the Christian because the latter does not understand the theory from which the secularist speaks. A course in systematic theology ought to do something to remedy this defect. Hence, this subsection on behaviorism.

John B. Watson is credited in this country with being the father of behaviorism, though, not to mention Nietzsche in Germany, William James in 1904 published an article, "Does Consciousness Exist?" to which he gave a negative answer.

Since the behaviorist position is fairly well known, it is neither necessary to describe it in great detail nor to refer to many authors. Briefly stated, behaviorism is the theory that souls or spirits do not exist, and that thinking, which they sometimes call mind, is a function of bodily parts in the same sense that digestion is the function of the stomach. The earlier identification of the bodily part as the larynx was soon discredited. A still very popular form of the theory makes thought a function of the brain. But a technically superior view makes thinking any muscular activity in general. All activities previously called mental are thus reduced to chemistry. Gilbert Ryle derides the idea of a soul as "the ghost in the machine," and classifies it as a "category mistake." B.F. Skinner can be characterized by the title of one of his chapters, "The World Within the Skin." The phrase occurs in other chapters as well. Contrasting the traditional view of perception with the view "common, I believe, to all versions of behaviorism" (*About Behaviorism,* New York, 1974, p. 73), he asserts that the former considers perception as active process, while the latter "is that the initiating action is taken by the environment rather than by the perceiver." But a warning is necessary. Readers who are unfamiliar with behavioristic authors may be deceived by their use of mentalistic terms such as feeling, pain, thinking, and even hunger, and other terms with similar connotations. Skinner is particularly guilty of this sort of deception. Of course he does not call it deception: Hunger is simply contractions of the stomach, and if thinking is not Watson's sub-vocal speech, it is still a complex of muscular motions.

Now, for one thing, this deceptive language disguises the fact that the behaviorists do not know what thinking is. To say that it is motion does not distinguish thought from digestion, or the emotion of fear from the solution of an equation. Had Skinner really tried to use literal language, had he confined himself to physical or physiological terminology, as behaviorism requires, his book would have been less clear and much less convincing.

Although Skinner and Ryle have had widespread influence, there was an earlier author who had much more and prepared the way for their successes. Because of the multiplicity of his publications and their multifaceted subject matter, not the least of which were his deleterious proposals on education, John Dewey is not usually classified in the narrower category of behaviorist. But he was a behaviorist nonetheless. Speaking of human habits he insists that "In the case of no other engine does one suppose that a defective machine will turn out goods simply because it is invited to. . . . Refusal to recognize this fact only leads to a separation of mind from body, and to supposing that mental or 'psychical' mechanisms are different in kind from those of bodily operations and independent of them" (*Human Nature and Conduct,* Henry Holt and Co., 1922, p. 33). Note the words *engine, machine, mechanisms, bodily operations.* Dewey teaches that knowledge resides in the muscles, that mental mechanisms are no different in kind from bodily operations.*

In another place Dewey insists that "Habits formed in the process of exercising biological aptitudes are the sole agents of observation, recollection, foresight, and judgment: a mind or consciousness or soul in general which performs these operations is a myth. . . . Knowledge which is not projected against the black unknown lives in the muscles." In fact, not even this statement is complete, for in *The Philosophy of John Dewey* (ed. Schlipp, p. 555) Dewey replies to his critics by saying, "Although the psychological theory involved is a form of behaviorism . . . behavior is not viewed as something taking

---

*Compare Clark, *Dewey* (Presbyterian and Reformed Publishing Co., 1960), pp. 53-61.

place under the skin . . . but always directly or indirectly in obvious overtness or at a distance . . . an interaction with environing conditions." In the same volume (p. 599) he replies to another critic: "There is no passage from the physical to the mental, from an external world to something felt. . . . When, however, a quality is termed a 'sensation'. . . it is now placed in a specially selected connection, that to the organism or self. Pending the outcome of an inquiry not yet completed, one may not know whether a quality, say red, belongs to *this* or *that* object in the environment, nor indeed whether it may not be the product of intraorganic processes as in the case of 'seeing stars' after a blow on the head. In other words, the occurrence of qualities upon my view is a purely natural event."

Behaviorism today permeates a large and important segment of society. A nurse in Detroit told me that she and the other nurses in the hospital, and the city policemen, were required to attend lectures advocating behaviorism.

Now, Christians should not sit idly by in ignorance or disinterest. But there are several ways of reacting. One is to preach the gospel without taking any notice of its antagonists. This is not what Paul did. Not only in I Corinthians and Galatians did he explicitly attack the enemies of Christ, but so also even in his shorter epistles. Yet not every sermon need be polemic. This present study itself, on the Biblical doctrine of man, could legitimately confine itself to exegesis. And surely it should not spend a hundred technical pages refuting behaviorism. Yet two or three pages seem called for.*

In keeping with the main purpose of this study, the reply will be first of all Biblical. Its basis will be the revealed truth that God is truth; he is a God of knowledge, and the Son is the Logos and Wisdom of God. Isaiah 33:6 says, "Wisdom and

---

*For a longer sample, compare Clark, *Behaviorism and Christianity* (Jefferson, Maryland: The Trinity Foundation, 1982).

knowledge shall be the stability of thy times and strength of salvation." Or in the New American Standard, "He shall be the stability of your times and a wealth of salvation, wisdom and knowledge." Of course behaviorists will not be impressed with any Scriptural dicta. If they were willing to take the time, they might well conclude that the orthodox doctrines are indeed what the Bible teaches, and that they are all nonsense. But they might be caught contradicting themselves if they say that the Bible is *all* nonsense. The vigor with which they press their theories indicates that they think that the philosophy of behaviorism is true, at least in the main. They believe that this life is all and enough, as Corliss Lamont claimed. That man is entirely physical or corporeal, they regard as true. They do not think that their theories are fundamentally false. In other words, they assert a difference between truth and falsehood.

But their assertion is inconsistent with their fundamental principle. Man is physics and chemistry, is he? Well, if a chemist combines hydrogen, sulphur, and oxygen, in certain proportions, he will have sulphuric acid. And to keep the examples elementary, if he combines sodium and chlorine, he will get salt. But is salt any more "true" than sulphuric acid? Make the example more complex. If certain brains and muscles perform motions called behaviorism, are they any more true than my brains and muscles whose intricate reaction is called Christianity? Reduce thinking to chemistry and no distinction between truth and error remains. Behaviorism has committed the suicide of self-contradiction.

Such a refutation is thoroughly Biblical; but in addition an illustration may be used which, though not in Scriptural language, nonetheless emphasizes the characteristics of truth versus the implications of behaviorism. It would be possible to reproduce a part of Plato's *Phaedo,* for several thinkers (only they could not admit to thinking) of that day held the same basic theory. But we shall begin with Leibniz and expand on him with a contemporary illustration.

Leibniz, in answer to the materialism or incipient behaviorism of his day, asked the reader to imagine the brain in a greatly enlarged form. Picture it in the dimensions of a large mill, so that one can walk into it and examine its machinery. We shall see, he says, bodily parts moving with bodily parts, as wheels turn wheels, but we shall never see a thought.

Leibniz's illustration can be improved, or at least up-dated, by using a baseball diamond, instead of a grist mill, as an illustration for the whole body, plus Dewey's distant objects, for the argument applies to any combination of moving parts. Accordingly the pitcher is one ganglionic cell, the catcher is a muscle in the leg, and the fielders are whatever you wish. Now, if thinking is a function of the brain, a particular thought must be a particular motion of one of the players. Let it be the curve of the opening pitch.

The first implication of this proposal is this: When the ball ends its motion in the catcher's mitt, that particular motion can never occur again. It is a past event. Similarly, if a thought is a motion in the body, that thought can never occur to you again. No one ever thinks the same thought twice.

The behaviorist or the baseball fan is likely to reply: True, the first pitch of the first inning cannot recur; but the pitcher will pitch his curve again in the third inning. Since the two curves are the same, the same thought can recur.

But this is not so easy as it seems. Aside from the admitted fact that the first thought cannot be thought again, we now ask, What is that thought of similarity by which you connect the first and third innings? How do you know the two curves are similar? The thought of similarity cannot be the first pitch because that was a thought about the hot dog vendor, or anything else, and was then similar to nothing, for no pitch preceded it. Nor can the thought of similarity be the curve in the third inning, because this pitch is supposedly similar to the hot dog vendor; and this man is surely not the idea of similarity.

Since, further, a thought of similarity or comparison cannot occur until there are two items to compare, the thought of similarity must be a later pitch—a fast ball in the fourth inning. Unfortunately the first pitch is over and gone in the fourth inning; so is the curve in the third. These pitches, i.e. these thoughts, these motions of bodily parts, are not present in the fourth inning, and hence the fast ball in the fourth cannot compare the previous pitches. Behaviorism makes comparison impossible; or, conversely, if comparison is possible, thinking cannot be a function of the brain.

Devastating as this may be, the argument does not end here. On the behavioristic view it is not only impossible for one person to have the same idea twice, but it is all the more impossible for two people to have the same thought once. If Pythagoras had the idea of a triangle, Einstein never learned Euclidean geometry. The ball park represents the person. One ball park is in Philadelphia, and we can call that person Pythagoras. Another ball park is in Chicago, and we may call that person Einstein. Tom, Dick, and Harry are in Birmingham, Baltimore, and Boston. Now, obviously the motion or thought, the act of digestion, that occurred on a certain date in one of these cities could not possibly recur in any other body. The wiggle of a dendritic process in my brain cannot be the wiggle in your brain. The motion of a bodily part cannot occur in two places, either at the same time or at different times. Therefore if J.B. Watson had some wiggles called the theory of behaviorism, I certainly do not have them. Nor could he know my refutation of behaviorism. I give it and hope it will be understood only because I do not regard thinking as a functioning of bodily parts.

Arguments from Leibniz or baseball are one way Christian academics can react to behaviorism. But what about the worshippers who sit in the pews every Lord's Day? Naturally the reactions of several million people will differ. But do those obdurately impractical "practical" Christians follow the argument? Note its implications concerning the other part of the image, to wit, righteousness. The logical positivists, who are a subdivision of behaviorism, abolish all morality along with the soul. The other behaviorists, Skinner for one, Dewey for another, very definitely want to reconstruct society. Christianity is a source of evil. It must be eradicated. Some form of socialism or communism can then impose a happy state of society. Prisons and penalties will be abolished because punishment is anti-social; parents will be prohibited from teaching their children religion, and capitalism will be destroyed. But if there is no truth, and if normative conclusions can never be deduced from observational premises, the politics of Dewey and Skinner have no basis except their own evil desires. As Supreme Court Justice Holmes wrote, "When one thinks coldly, I can see no reason for attributing to man a significance different in kind from that which belongs to a baboon or to a grain of sand. . . . I wonder if cosmically an idea is any more important than the bowels." In an article, "Hobbes, Holmes, and Hitler," Ben W. Palmer quotes Holmes as saying, "I am so skeptical as to our knowledge about the goodness and badness of laws that I have no practical criterion except what the crowd wants." Palmer concluded that this Supreme Court Justice's theory was indistinguishable from that of a storm trooper proclaiming the supremacy of the blonde beast.* No wonder

---

*Compare Clark, *A Christian View of Men and Things* (Jefferson, Maryland: The Trinity Foundation, 1991 [1952]), p. 11.

that the present Court initiated the murder of millions of innocent babies. That seems to be what the crowd wants. Devotional, emotional, practical anti-intellectual Christianity, if indeed it is Christianity, cannot meet present realities.

7. Dichotomy and Trichotomy

The previous sections have interpreted the Bible as teaching that God is truth and that man is rational. The immediately preceding section defended the distinction between truth and falsehood, and the spirituality of man against the major contemporary attack on Christianity. Important, yes; fundamental as these points are, Genesis gives further details relative to man's nature. These too have implications for soteriology and therefore cannot be omitted. Since God is rational, his revelation is systematic, and his faithful servants are obligated to study the interrelationships to the best of their individual abilities.

Up to this point emphasis has been put on man's soul or mind, for surely this is the basic truth about man's nature. However, man also has a body. An earlier page mentioned some theologians who, in the interest of man's unity, somewhat made man a compound like NaCl. This, I hold, is not the Biblical view, but of course man does have a body and what the Bible says on the subject must not be ignored. In fact some theologians, instead of considering man in his present compound state as body and soul, advocate a threefold division. They say that man is three-fold, like H_2SO_4. He is a compound of body, soul, and spirit. The theological terminology for these two views is dichotomy and trichotomy.

Before the Biblical documentation is spread on the page, a very slight bit of history will provide an elementary perspective. Yet one must be cautious. Keep in mind that the church did not succeed in formulating the doctrine of the Trinity until A.D. 325. Other doctrines remained in confusion. Note too that the modern theologians sometimes fail to understand second and third century language, not to mention their distortions of Greek philosophy. Several of them assign a Logos doctrine to Plato, though actually it is Stoic. Many have found references to Gnosticism in the New Testament, and they describe it as a dualistic system. This latter is a mistake that should not have been made even in the nineteenth century. Since the middle of the twentieth century, with new discoveries, one can plausibly or even confidently say that the New Testament shows no, or only the slightest, knowledge of Gnosticism. Since the problem of man's prelapsarian composition is by no means so important as the Trinity, the very early views of the subject abound in confusion.

It is true that some early theologians held a sort of trichotomy. But the view shortly disappeared. The reason was that Apollinaris, a contemporary of Athanasius, used the doctrine to produce a defective Christology. The Nicene Council had concluded nothing as to the relationship between the divine and the human natures of Christ. Clearly this is a matter of interest, and a difficult one. Apollinaris was no Arian; he sincerely accepted the deity of Christ; but he could not handle Christ's humanity. Instead of attributing to Christ what was later called "a reasonable soul," he allowed him only an "animal" soul, and substituted the divine Logos for the other.*

Parenthetically, one of those modern theologians who does not understand all he knows described some of the ancient views as giving Christ or man three souls: nutritive,

---

*Compare W.G.T. Shedd, *A History of Christian Doctrine*, Vol. 1, pp. 394 ff.

animal, and rational. The division is Aristotle's, but it does not imply that animals have two souls and man three. The soul or living principle of plants is nutritive only. The soul of what we now call animals has two functions: nutrition and sensation. Man's soul is as unitary as one can wish, but it has three functions. Apollinaris denied the third function to Christ's soul, substituting, as was said above, the thoroughly divine Logos. But the church at large, however confusedly, recognized that the Atonement required a man. Hence not only was Apollinaris condemned, but trichotomy also died out. This is not to say that all trichotomists deny the humanity of Christ: The above is history, not necessarily logic.

Trichotomy remained in its tomb until resurrected in the nineteenth century by several English and German theologians. Hodge pays some slight attention to this movement (II, pp. 47 ff., 400ff.), but Laidlaw complains that Hodge considered trichotomy only in its crudest form (p. 68, and footnote 2); but as its crudest form alone has currency in this twentieth century, this study will merit the same criticism. So far as I know, the authors whom Laidlaw so competently discussed now have no descendents, though basic trichotomy enjoys a measure of popularity.

It would be tedious and time consuming to quote every verse in the Bible that in some way or other bears on the subject. But it is imperative that a fair amount of documentation be laid down as a foundation. Though the present writer makes no apologies for several pages which to some people seem too philosophic and secular, he insists that the foundation is always the Scripture. As one must suppose, it begins in the first chapter of Genesis.

Genesis 2:7   And the Lord God formed man of the
                     dust of the ground, and breathed into

	his nostrils the breath of life, and man became a living soul.
Genesis 3:19	Dust thou art, and unto dust shalt thou return.
Ecclesiastes 12:7	the dust returneth to the earth as it was, and the spirit returneth unto God who gave it.
Isaiah 10:18	both soul and body
Daniel 7:15	my spirit was grieved in the midst of my body . . .
Matthew 6:25	Be not anxious for your life . . . nor yet for your body . . . Is not the life more than the food, and the body more than the raiment?
Matthew 10:28	Be not afraid of them that kill the body, but are not able to kill the soul; but rather fear him who is able to destroy both soul and body in hell.
Luke 10:27	Thou shalt love the Lord thy God with all thy heart and with all thy soul and with all thy strength and with all thy mind.
I Thessalonians 5:23	The very God of peace sanctify you wholly; and may your spirit, soul, and body be preserved complete.
Hebrews 4:12	piercing even to the dividing asunder of soul and spirit and of the joints and marrow.

Since Genesis describes the creation of man, there is no better place to look in order to determine his components. Genesis 2:7 mentions the body, the dust of the ground. On this point there is no dispute. Everybody agrees that Adam had a body. Genesis next mentions the breath of God. The Hebrew word is *neshamah*. It means a blast of wind, even destructive in force; not just a gentle breathing as one might imagine from the context. The word *ruach* (spirit) is what we could have expected, from its occurrence in Genesis 1:2 where the verb *moved* is not particularly violent. But at any rate in Genesis 2:7 we have a body, a blast of wind, and a *nephesh,* or as translated in the King James, a living soul.

The point to notice here is that God constructed man out of two elements: the dust of the ground and his own breath. The combination is the *nephesh.* A parallel illustration may be of help. Suppose, under proper laboratory conditions, I mix some sodium with some chlorine and the mixture becomes salt. Salt is not one of the elements: it is the name of the compound. So also in Genesis: God took some clay, breathed his spirit into it, and the combination was a living soul. In the Old Testament the term *soul* designates the combination as a whole, not just one of the components.

Several distinguished theologians are in complete agreement. John Gill, though not belaboring the point as if to refute someone, expresses the dichotomous view as obvious from Scripture. Admittedly I do not agree with him that the image is "the whole man, both body and soul" (*Body of Divinity,* III, iv, pp. 274, 275); but he adds on the same page, "The principal seat of the image of God in man is the soul." The pertinent point at the moment is that he describes the whole man as "soul and body." He had already said, "the constituent and essential parts of man . . . are two, body and soul" (p. 270). There is not the least bit of trichotomy. Since Gill is so frequently prolix, one is tempted to guess that he had never heard of trichotomy. A second historical note is the material from Oehler-Day (*Old Testament Theology,* New York, 1883, pp. 149-152); and though it is not so decisive or blunt as the chemical illustrations, it fairly well substantiates dichotomy. Hodge, for another reference (*Systematic Theology,* II, p. 48) clearly says "There is in this account no intimation of anything more than the material body . . . and the living principle derived from God."

In this same place Hodge refutes an idea frequently asserted by trichotomists. They hold that man is composed of body, soul, and spirit. Soul is earthbound and is common to man and animals, but spirit is the consciousness of God which no animal has. In addition to what anyone can find out by reading an English Bible, namely that the term *spirit* is assigned to animals as well as to men, Hodge compares a number of passages to show that *nephesh* and *ruach* are synonyms and interchangeable. Genesis 6:17, 7:15, 22, and Ecclesiastes 3:21 all apply the word *spirit* to animals. Of course men are conscious of God, but if *spirit* is defined as God-consciousness, we ought to follow the example of St. Francis and preach the gospel to the birds.

To return to the list of quoted verses, Genesis 3:19, Ecclesiastes 12:7, Isaiah 10:18, and Daniel 7:15 all clearly support dichotomy. The verse in Isaiah is puzzling, for it specifies *nephesh* and body, the compound with a component. A two fold division is perfectly clear, but it is not the division found in Genesis. One must remember, however, that the colloquial language of the Bible is not the technical terminology of a persnickety theologian. I take it as a literary emphasis, as if a gangster should yell "I'll kill you dead and smash your head in." Surely Isaiah did not intend to contradict Genesis.

So much then for the Old Testament. In addition to the few New Testament verses in the last list, three more may now be added, with a comment. Matthew 26:38 describes the soul as sorrowful, and John 13:21 says the spirit is sad. Apparently soul and spirit can be used synonymously. Matthew 10:28 in the previous list speaks of soul and body; James 2:26 has spirit and body. In each case the entire person is meant. Luke 1:46, 47 and Philippians 1:27 both combine soul and spirit. This is literary parallelism. If anyone doubts it, the more important passages can be adduced.

These more explicit passages invite a direct confrontation with the most popular form of twentieth century trichotomy. It is the trichotomy of the Scofield Bible and the theology of Lewis Sperry Chafer. Although some of the members of the present Dallas Seminary faculty have modified the earlier position of the school and have published a new edition of the Scofield Bible, deleting some of the original notes, the original position is a fact of history and still remains the view of many ministers and many church members. A charge of misrepresentation is therefore inapplicable.

The Scofield Bible's note on I Thessalonians 5:23 reads in part, "Man is a trinity. That the human soul and spirit are not identical is proved by the facts that they are divisible (Hebrews 4:22), and that the soul and spirit are sharply distinguished in the burial and resurrection of the body . . . I Corinthians 15:44. . . . The distinction is that the spirit is that part of the body . . . which 'knows' (I Corinthians 2:11), his mind; the soul is the seat of his *affections, desires,* and so of the *emotions,* and of the active *will,* the self. . . . The word translated 'soul' (*nephesh*) in the O.T. is the exact equivalent of the N.T. word for soul (Grk. *psuchē*) and the use of 'soul' in the O.T. is identical with the use of that word in the N.T. (see, e.g. Deuteronomy 6:5; 14:26) . . . . Because man is 'spirit' he is capable of God-consciousness . . . because he is 'soul' he has self-consciousness, . . . because he is 'body' he has, through his senses, world-consciousness."

As for I Thessalonians 5:23 itself ("may your spirit and soul and body be preserved entire"), one can note that if this teaches trichotomy, then Jesus contradicted it and in Matthew 22:37 asserted four elements in man's make-up. The body, which he did not mention, and three others, heart, soul, and mind. Spirit is not included in the list. Deuteronomy 6:5, which the verse in Matthew echoes, has *might,* instead of *mind*; and Luke 10:27, the parallel passage, enumerates four "elements," with the body as an unexpressed fifth. One may therefore wonder why I Thessalonians 5:23 was selected as the decisive verse on the composition of man.

Naturally some of Scofield's statements are true enough, though not always in the sense he intended. For example, it is true that the human soul and spirit, as these words are used in the Old Testament, "are not identical." At least they are not always identical. In fact they are often, even usually, synonymous. But far from proving that man is a trinity, the statement that they are not identical remains true when *spirit* is an element and *soul* the compound. Furthermore, Scofield is mistaken when he says that "The word tr. 'soul' (*nephesh*) in the Old Testament is the exact equivalent of the N.T. word for soul (Gk. *psuchē*)." Why they are not exact equivalents will be explained later. Because they are not, the Scofield reference to I Corinthians 15:44 requires an amount of exegesis. Again, to say that the soul, as opposed to the spirit, is the seat of affections or emotions contradicts I Kings 21:5, "Why is thy spirit so sad?" Scofield also says that the soul (emotion and will), not the spirit (the mind or intellect) is the self. Hodge seems to agree when he says (*Systematic Theology,* Vol. II, p. 48), "The soul is the man himself, that in which his identity and personality reside: It is the *Ego.*" But there is no real agreement because Hodge identifies soul and spirit, while Scofield "sharply distinguished" them. The subject is somewhat more complex than it seems at first; and hence more detailed and penetrating discussion is needed.

Certain cautions are to be observed in this discussion. Some Christian writers take pleasure in emphasizing the unity of man as opposed to "Greek dualism," or Cartesian dualism. Now, virtually every thinker who has discussed the nature of man has asserted his unity, and also some sort of duality. Even Spinoza had a dualism, a very prominent dualism. This is not the problem. The problem is posed by asking: what sort of unity and what sort of duality? Plato indeed had a duality of an everlasting though derivative soul and an everlasting underived chaotic space, out of which latter the human body was formed. Obviously this is not Christian. But Descartes asserted the creation of two different substances, soul and body; and many orthodox theologians would consider this quite Christian. This is not to say that Descartes used the term *anima* in the same sense that Moses used the word *nephesh*. In these discussions one must always take care to determine the precise meaning of the author, for the usages of various authors vary. And while the meanings of the words *unity* and *duality* may be the same to many authors, the nature of the unity and duality often varies greatly.

Scriptural language is the common popular language of the time. The Bible, especially the Old Testament, does not use many fixed technical terms. Soul and flesh are synonymous in Job 13:14, 14:22, and in Psalms 63:1. Heart and mind, referring to God, are synonymous in I Samuel 2:35; flesh and heart in Proverbs 14:30, Ecclesiastes 2:3, 11:10, and Ezekiel 44:7, 9 (though in Ezekiel a distinction could be asserted). Soul, heart, and flesh seem to be identical in Psalm 84:2; heart and flesh in Psalm 16:9; soul and spirit are parallel in Isaiah 26:9; and much to our elementary confusion Psalm 31:9 combines eye, soul, and belly.

The New Testament also uses the same popular language in many places. A moment ago it was said that Scofield contradicts I Kings 21:5 because there the spirit is sad. In John 13:21 it is the *spirit* that is troubled, though in Matthew 26:38, as in Psalm 42:11, it is the *soul* that is sorrowful. In Matthew 10:28 "soul and body" means the entire man; in James 2:26 the entire man is "spirit and body."

When the Virgin Mary in Luke 1:46, 47—a passage penetrated with Old Testament piety—referred to her soul and spirit, she was using the language of the Psalms, where soul and spirit are synonymous and parallel. But generally in the New Testament *psuchē* and *pneuma* are not parallel.

Though both Testaments regularly use popular imprecise language, the New differs from the Old by introducing something more technical. The Apochrypha and Philo used the terms *soul* and *spirit* with greater attention to psychological niceties. Their phraseology filtered down into the common speech. The New Testament uses these terms, then, in a way somewhat different from the parallelism of the Psalms, while also reflecting the older usage. The difference in usage is more clear and consistent with the adjectives *soulish* and *spiritual*, than with the nouns. In James 3:15 there is a wisdom that is "earthly, *soulish,* demonic." Jude 19 speaks of men who are *soulish,* not having spirit." See also I Corinthians 2:14, 15:44, and Philippians 3:20.

Nor does the word *flesh* in the New Testament regularly denote the body or dust of Genesis. Flesh, like soul, often refers to man's sinful nature. Spirit or spiritual does not designate the breath of God as one of the two elements in man's make-up, nor even his mind in a simple psychological sense, but rather, when it does not mean the Holy Spirit himself, it designates a man who is under the Spirit's beneficent control.

Now, the theory of trichotomy comes in various forms. Scofield's is about the most superficial and simplistic one can find. Others develop a complex psychology, a theory of regeneration, or an application to Christ's incarnate nature. This was true of Apollinaris briefly mentioned above. Because of Apollinaris, trichotomy disappeared until in 1769 it reappeared in a book by M.F. Roos. This gentleman was a careful scholar and avoided later extremisms by refusing to go much beyond a study of the usage of the terms. Olshausen (1834) proposed an embryonic psychology, hardly as definite as that of Apollinaris. Delitzsch goes a little further. Soul and spirit, he says, are two substances, but one in nature, as the Son and Spirit are one in nature, but two hypostases. His analogies, as analogies usually, are not enlightening: The body is the house of the soul, and the soul is the house of the spirit; or, the soul is related to the triune nature. Delitzsch as a good scholar acknowledges that the Bible contains many dichotomous passages. In fact he is so honest in this that he virtually contradicts himself.

J.B. Heard, *Tripartite Nature,* worked out a much more complete scheme of trichotomy and integrated it with his doctrines of sin and redemption, or vice versa. Man is a tripartite hypostasis, he says; i.e. a person with three natures or possibly composed of three substances. Soul was created free to choose either the direction of the body or the direction of the spirit. Adam chose the body. Consequently his descendants inherited a deadened spirit. This trichotomous view, held by the Greek Fathers, never penetrated the Latin mind, Heard complains, and the results were Augustine's unacceptable refutation of Pelagius and the defective view of sin held by the Reformers. If man is bipartite and if sin is positive, like a virus, either human recuperative powers would have destroyed the virus or the virus would have, by this time, destroyed the race. But if sin is negative, then the bipartite theory results in Pelagianism. The solution is: Sin is negative, but man is a trinity. The result of the fall, an event far more serious than Pelagius allowed, but not so serious as Augustine thought, is a deadened spirit. Original sin is thus privative only, though a serious privation. Since the spirit is only deadened, not annihilated, there is a possibility of regeneration. On the bipartite view regeneration would be impossible. So also sanctification. If the soul were thoroughly corrupt—and man had no spirit—the Holy Spirit could not purify the soul; but in the tripartite scheme the soul remains prone to evil, but the regenerated spirit cannot sin.*

What should be noted in this subject is its effect on many other doctrines. It is not just a detached piece of psychology. The nature of Christ is affected; the role of the Holy Spirit is affected; as also regeneration and sanctification. What a seminary student must learn and keep in mind, and what ninety-nine percent of the communicant members never consider, is that Christianity is a *system* of doctrine. Truth forms a system. Doctrines interlock; and as J. Gresham Machen used to say, most people are saved by blessed inconsistency.

One further Scriptural passage, though of lesser importance, can serve as a closing paragraph for this section. Hebrews 4:12, "dividing asunder of soul and spirit, and of the joints and marrow," is sometimes quoted to sustain a division between soul and spirit. The verse, however, does not say that soul and spirit are two of the elements out of which man was composed. But what is even more to the point, the basic division in this verse is not three-fold but two-fold: soul and spirit versus joints and marrow. If, now, soul and spirit are two different components, then joints and marrow must also be another two; and man is four-fold, not tripartite. Further, the excellence of Christ (not the written word: compare John Owen's comentary on Hebrews) is that he can divide what is seemingly indivisible. If soul and spirit were as sharply distin-

---

*This is a very brief summary of Laidlaw's detailed analysis.

guished as the trichotomists say, the ability to divide them would not be a noteworthy excellence of Christ. The verse therefore closely conjoins them, and in this instance too it favors dichotomy.

8. Traducianism and Creationism

The next question concerns the origin of the souls of Adam's descendants. Do the children inherit, derive, or get their souls from their parents (traducianism), or does God perform an act of creation for every baby?

The theory of creationism maintains that God immediately creates *ex nihilo* a new soul for each individual. Some verses that seem to favor this view are:

Numbers 16:22	And they fell upon their faces, and said, O God, the God of the spirits of all flesh, shall one man sin, and wilt thou be wroth with all the congregation?
Psalm 33:15	He fashioneth their hearts alike; he considereth all their works.
Isaiah 57:16	For I will not contend for ever, neither will I be always wroth; for the spirit should fail before, and the souls which I have made.
Jeremiah 38:16	As the Lord liveth, that made us this soul . . .
Zechariah 12:1	The burden of the word of the Lord for Israel, saith the Lord, which stretcheth forth the heavens, and layeth the foundation of the earth, and formeth the spirit of man within him.

These verses are hardly conclusive, for they do not specify an immediate creation rather than an extended process. Of course there is other material also. Let us then see what some theologians do with it.

The great Baptist theologian, John Gill, argues as follows in his *Body of Divinity* (III,3). Christ, he reminds us, was made like us in all ways except sin, and therefore had a true body and a reasonable soul. This soul, Gill insists, could not have come from Mary, for as a sinner she would have transmitted a sinful soul. This argument, however, depends on some doubtful assumptions. If the soul of the child comes from the father, and the body from the mother, as some earlier theologians had it, Gill's reference to Mary would be beside the point. Maybe the notion that the father alone propagates the soul is mere superstition; but until Gill proves the contrary, his argument is defective.

What may more disturb those who wish to stay close to the Bible is the similarity between Gill's argument and the Romanists' defense of the immaculate conception of Mary. The argument founders because the difficulty reappears with Mary's mother. How could the sinful mother of Mary produce a sinless daughter? If God could so control the conception of Mary, and produce a sinless girl from a sinful parent, why is it impossible that this is what he did in the incarnation, rather than a generation earlier?

Of course this absurdity of Romanism does not attach to Gill. He holds that if the soul comes from the parent, the new soul just could not possibly be sinless. Hence, it must have been created *ex nihilo*. Yet the miracle, if it be a miracle at all, of producing a sinless soul from a sinful parent, is nothing in comparison with the most stupendous miracle of all: not just the virgin birth, but the incarnation itself. If the eternal God can become incarnate, surely the lesser miracle need not trouble us. Even so, and in conjunction with the federal headship of Adam, one would like to know how Jesus could have been born sinless.

There is a reasonable, or at least a possible explanation. The imputation of Adam's guilt, not Eve's previous sin, may be based on the male line. If so, the virgin birth would avoid the imputation of guilt to, and the consequent corruption of, a son so born.

Gill also argues that souls are incapable of producing other souls. His reason for saying so is that angels are souls, and angels do not propagate. The argument is an obvious fallacy because the undistributed term *souls* in the minor premise is distributed in the conclusion. The syllogistic form is: no angels propagate; all angels are souls; therefore no souls propagate. EAE in the third figure is invalid. No third figure syllogism has a universal conclusion.

Again Gill argues that the soul of the child could not come from a part of the parent's soul, for souls have no parts. But if it came from the whole of the parent's soul, the parent would have no soul left and his body would immediately die. This is ludicrous. Traducianism does not assert that the parent's soul becomes the child's soul, but that the parent's soul produces another soul for the child. That souls have no parts, at least in any spatial sense, must be maintained. But souls have functions. They are active. Why cannot one produce another? This of course is speculation: It does not prove traducianism. What it does is to show that Gill's argument is equally speculation and fallacious to boot.

Gill's clinching argument is based on Hebrews 12:9, "We had the fathers of our flesh to chasten us . . . shall we not much rather be in subjection to the Father of spirits." His point is that the immediate source of our flesh or body is our earthly parents, and therefore the immediate source of our spirit is God the Father. Yet in the same paragraph Gill admits that a parent horse generates the colt's spirit. John Owen has the same interpretation, though he does not mention horses. The opposing theologians would point out that the context is a discussion of chastisement. The main point is that as we reverenced the fathers of our flesh when they chastened us, we should all the more be in subjection to the Father of spirits. The text does not read "the Father of our spirits," though obviously we are individually included with all other Christians. But the exegesis of Gill and Owen depends on inserting the word, or idea, *immediate* before the words *fathers* and *Father*. This idea cannot be read into the text as the previous word *our* can. In fact the word *father* itself does not have the same connotation in both instances. There are many differences—and this puts it mildly—between our Father in heaven and our earthly father. Therefore creationism is at best nothing more than a possible interpretation. The verse does not deny creationism; nor does it assert traducianism; it is simply silent on the question.

Archibald Alexander Hodge, in his truly magnificent volume on *The Atonement,* defends creationism as necessary to a proper understanding of that central doctrine of Christianity. The problem A.A. Hodge faces is the relationship between Adam's first sin and the guilt of the human race. What is behind the phrase, "In Adam all die?" How could Adam's descendants be personally guilty and merit God's punishment? Hodge objects to the Realism of W.G.T. Shedd, whom he represents as saying (not a verbatim quotation from Shedd) that "Adam was the entire *genus homo*, as well as the first individual . . . every individual member [of the human race] was physically and numerically one with him . . . hence the whole genus is guilty. . . . This is the Realistic view recently advocated . . . by Dr. William G.T. Shedd" (p. 99). On the next two pages he reiterates the idea that we "were *really* and *numerically* one with Adam" and that "this Realistic theory of our *numerical* oneness with Adam is an essential element of the doctrine. . . ."

In these and his following pages Hodge seems to labor under two important misconceptions. He is quite convinced that traducianism, a theory concerning the propagation of the soul, is utterly inconsistent with the doctrines of federal headship and immediate imputation. This just is not so. There is no logical incongruity between the proposition, the souls of descendants are propagated through their parents, and the proposition, Adam acted as the legal representative for all men. Rather, is it not plausible that the first propagator would be the best representative? In fact, Hodge agrees with this last plausibility (*ibid.*, p. 111), but he seems unaware how much this undermines his arguments against traducianism.

Then, second, Hodge seems to have a defective view of Realism. Realism of course asserts the real existence of the human genus. This is an Idea in God's mind and it is a real object of knowledge. But it is hard to imagine any Realist identifying the perfect eternal Idea with a temporal and imperfect individual. The relationship of Adam to the Idea is precisely the same as the relationship of any other individual man to the Idea. The individuals "participate" in, or are all "patterned after" the Idea; but the notion that one individual is "physically and numerically one" with the Idea, or that any other individual is "physically and numerically one" with Adam is enough to send poor Plato to his grave in despair. This misunderstanding of Realism vitiates much of Hodge's argumentation.

We may admit that some of Shedd's expressions are imprecise. He does not pin down the nature of the unity between Adam and the Idea. He uses the phrase "the Adamic existence and unity" (*History of Doctrine,* II, p.16); and also "the Adamic unity in respect to both body and soul" (*ibid.*, p. 24). Later he asserts that the Latin fathers held that "man was created as a species, in respect of both soul and body" (*ibid.*, p.91); these phrases may be imprecise, but they do not support Hodge's assertions. There must be some sort of Adamic existence and unity; this unity surely has something to do with both body and soul; and the species man was eternally in God's mind as truly as Adam was created. But these indubitable truths do not justify an assertion of the *numerical* and *physical* unity of each human being with Adam. Could Shedd or anyone else ever have held that I am physically and numerically Adam, and that you are too, and that therefore you and I are the numerically identical body now sitting in this chair? Furthermore, A.A. Hodge cites no page on which Shedd makes such an assertion.

There is a passage in Augustine that asserts a peculiar unity of all men, including Adam, with a generic human nature. The translation of the *City of God* (XIII, 14) in the Post-Nicene Fathers seems to say that this generic unity sinned before Adam sinned. To quote, "Man . . . begot corrupted and condemned children. For we all were in that one man, since we all were that one man, who fell into sin by the woman. . . . For not yet was the particular form created and distributed to us, in whom we as individuals were to live, but already the seminal nature was there. . . ."

But the 1947 reprint of the Healey translation in Everyman's Library has it differently. The important sentences are these: "For in him were we all, since we all were that one man, who . . . fell into sin. We had not our particular forms yet, but there was the seed of our natural propagation, which being corrupted by sin must produce man of that same nature. . . ."

The only phrase that could offend contemporary nominalists is, "we all were that one man." But nothing in the text defines that unity as numerical. The text says indeed that the seed of our natural propagation was in Adam; and in that sense we were physically in Adam. Who can deny it? The text also says that our present corrupt nature is inherited from our parents. If creationism is correct, then we do not inherit our corruption from our parents, but we get it immediately from God in his creative act. Can this be the Biblical position?

Even Hodge does not want to say that God creates depraved souls. In his catechetical *Outlines of Theology* (p. 349) he writes, "(1) God cannot be the author of sin. (2) We must not believe that he could consistently with his own perfections create a creature *de novo* with a sinful nature." But whether the first paragraph on 352 implies that children are born sinless, is a question its language does not answer clearly.

One may well suspect that Hodge gives away his case, when in *The Atonement* (p. 114) he admits, "If, on the other hand, the question be asked *HOW* inherent moral corruption originates in a newly-created soul and yet the Creator of the soul be not the author of the sin, it must be confessed in reply that the Scriptures give us no direct solution, and that various answers have been given by men equally orthodox."

May we then conclude (1) that the inability of creationism to absolve God of the immediate creation of sinful souls is a point against creationism; (2) that propagation by parents is a very natural and plausible assumption; (3) that traducianism does not conflict with immediate imputation and the federal headship of Adam; and (4) not only divine immutability in general, but the specific statement that God rested from his work of creation renders incredible the notion that God issued many billions of creative fiats after the original creative week.

Both Hodges confidently claim that creationism has been the majority opinion among Reformed theologians. Is it possible to detect a fissure in this granite mass? Louis Berkof, and of course all Dutch theologians are incurably Reformed, in his *Systematic Theology* (pp. 196 ff.), discusses the two views. He notes that there was some traducianism in the early church (e.g. Tertullian, Leo the Great), but that creationism eventually became the dominant opinion, as in Thomas Aquinas and Peter Lombard. Luther and his successors favored traducianism, but Calvinists "decidedly favored creationism."

Yet Berkhof, after giving the arguments pro and con, does not accept creationism as whole-heartedly as its better known exponents do. He rather straddles the issue. The closing paragraph (p. 201) gives three reasons for preferring creationism, but then he adds, "At the same time we are convinced that the creative activity of God in originating human souls must be conceived as being most closely connected with the natural process in the generation of new individuals. Creationism does not claim to be able to clear up all the difficulties, but at the same time it serves as a warning against [certain] errors. . . ."

Although creationism justly claims to be the view of the majority of Calvinists, there have been dissenters. Berkhof mentions H.B. Smith, W.G.T. Shedd, and, though not so Calvinistic, A.H. Strong. Hence if the arguments above are inconclusive, and some outright fallacies, it is time to give something in support of traducianism. Perhaps they too may prove inconclusive, and if so, one can rely only on probability. Yet I think one of them is more than merely probable. It will be the first to be stated.

Traducianism holds that children derive not only their bodies from their parents, but their souls also. It sees no reason why there should be many billions of creative acts for souls, when one act of creation was suffcient for all bodies. This is not a mere supposition. It seems to have incontestable Scriptural support. Genesis 2:2, 3 says that God rested from his work of creation, and the Sabbath was instituted to commemorate his resting. There is no hint that God ever created anything again.

Then, of course, though it is a subsidiary point, the creationists can only squirm at the inference that God immediately created sinful souls.

Finally, and this too is subsidiary, verses in which God refers to "the souls which I have made," if taken in the creationist sense, would imply that God immediately created the trees on my lawn. They are indeed a part of creation, but immediately they grew from the seeds of previous trees. The conclusion is, to put it modestly, that traducianism is well nigh inescapable.

9. Adam and the Fall: The Covenant of Works

Most of the preceding has dealt with man's basic nature as created. It has been impossible to exclude all references to sin and its effects, but the topic was restricted to a minimum. Now the argument must proceed to what happened next. There will be a brief résumé of Adam's original nature and then a description of the changes that took place. The brief résumé must begin with Adam's rationality, for this has a great deal to do with his relationship to God.

The section on the image of God showed that mankind was created rational. Although sin and salvation have been anticipated, the main line of development has come only to man's dichotomous composition and the propagation of the soul. Therefore we return to Adam. Created as an adult, his intellect was ready for the problems that faced him. Among them was the necessity of talking with Eve, and especially of talking with God. Since God obviously intended to speak to men, Adam must have had from the first an ability to understand and reply.

Genesis 1:28, 29	And God blessed them, and God said unto them, Be fruitful, and multiply, and replenish the earth, . . . and have dominion . . . over every living thing that moveth upon the earth.
Genesis 2:16, 17	And the Lord God commanded the man, saying, Of every tree of the garden thou mayest freely eat: But of the tree of the knowledge of good and evil, thou shalt not eat of it: for in the day that thou eatest thereof thou shalt surely die.
Genesis 2:19, 20	And out of the ground the Lord God formed every beast of the field, . . . and brought them unto Adam to see what he would call them: . . . And Adam gave names to all cattle, . . . , and to every beast of the field.

This is not to say that Adam was created with a complete vocabulary. Nor had he developed Newtonian calculus. But he had enough vocabulary to understand what God said to him and enough intellectual ingenuity to invent names or symbols for the animals.

The problem of language is a difficult one for secular philosophers. Rousseau recognized the paradox he faced. To learn a language, one must live in a society that speaks the language, as a baby does; but for a society to exist, it is first necessary that they speak a common language. After Rousseau, the evolutionists tried to develop language out of the grunts of pigs and the twittering of birds. Wilbur Marshall Urban placed emphasis on the imitation of natural sounds. He cites a so-called primitive language in which two or three similar syllables are supposed to sound like a murmuring brook; then with two more of the same syllables the word means *ocean.* The meanings are supposedly conveyed by the sound itself. It is not likely that anyone could guess the meaning of the first word; and what is worse onomatopoeia does not account for words such as *because, the, left, therefore, seven,* or even *agricola* and *georgos.*

Furthermore, evolution requires simplicity at the start and complexity later on; but the older known languages are all more complex than the modern languages. Latin is tremendously more complicated than French, and the savage languages are worse than Latin.

While this is an embarrassment to evolutionary theories, it does not follow that Adam invented or was endowed with the most complicated grammar ever used; for the confusion of tongues at Babel broke the continuity of linguistic development, and we today have no idea of what Adam's language was. But that he spoke a rational language immediately is a clear inference from Genesis. He was created rational for the purpose of speaking to God and to Eve.

With respect to Adam's original state, and particularly the image of God, the Greek theologians imagined that they completely excluded Adam's moral conformity from the image. Some Lutherans, in order to stress original righteousness and its loss in the fall, seem to exclude rationality and restrict the image to Adam's moral nature. The Reformed theologians often say they include both. But this way of stating the matter is awkward. Both Lutherans and Calvinists speak as if rationality and morality are quite distinct. It is better, however, to recognize that morality is a subdivision of rationality. Conscience, whether perfect or defiled, is not a separate element in man's constitution. It is simply the human activity of thinking about moral norms. Man thinks of arithmetic and he thinks of obeying God's commands. Adam before the fall thought correctly about both subjects. He was indeed altogether righteous, but he was so because he was altogether rational. As Charles Hodge says (*Systematic Theology,* II, p.99), in a few lines that are almost a verbatim quotation from Thomas Aquinas (*Summa Theologica,* I, Q. 95, 1) "His reason was subject to God; his will was subject to his reason; his affections and appetites to his will; the body was the obedient organ of the soul."

This picture of man is quite different from the one Aristotle gives us. Of course there was no first man for Aristotle: He taught that the human race had always lived on the planet Earth. Neither did Aristotle have the Hebrew-Christian concept of sin and its disastrous effects. But aside from these two points the basic difference in ethics is that for Aristotle each man is born morally neutral (and had there been a first man, he too would have been morally neutral). As the child grows, he learns to live morally, or immorally, by practice. It is similar to learning the piano. If the child practices the correct fingering, he will develop good habits and in time play Mozart's sonatas smoothly. But if he makes a mistake in fingering, and repeats the mistake, he will soon develop bad habits that can hardly, if ever, be corrected. This is not the Biblical view of man, either before or after the fall. Man was not created neutral: He was positively righteous. After the fall men are born totally depraved. In neither case is man morally neutral. Although the Roman church, in adopting Aristotle as its patron philosopher, never copied this theory of ethics completely, Aristotle's influence on Romanism produced a view of sin and regeneration that is quite different from what the Bible teaches.

The Romanists acknowledge that Adam before the fall was as a matter of fact rational and righteous. So far as this fact is concerned they do not differ from the Protestant view. But whereas the Protestants include the righteousness in the image of God, the Romanists restrict the image to the natural powers of reason, and then they consider righteousness as an additional supernatural gift. In the fall, man loses his original righteousness, but retains the image in its completeness.

If this should seem to be "merely" a difference in the usage of the term *image* (for the Protestants also say that righteousness was lost but reason retained), one may reply that a Christian theologian should use Biblical terms in their Biblical meaning. One may also reply that, as in the case of *justification* also, the non-biblical usage results in an unbiblical doctrine of sin and salvation.

This becomes clear when the Romanists assert that the body and the spirit, before the fall, had, not merely diverse, but actually contrary inclinations. These inclinations fought: *Ex his autem diversis, vel contrariis propensionitus existere in unoeodem homine pugnam quantam* (Bellarmin, *De Gratia Primi Hominis*).

This theory is not explicit in the Decrees of Trent. These are deliberately obscure; and any Reformer could perfectly well accept most of the wording of the Fifth Session on original sin. There is one sentence, however, that the Reformers could not accept. Our catechism says that sin is any want of conformity unto, as well as transgression of the law of God. But the Decrees of Trent refuse to make the lack of conformity truly and properly sin. The text is, "in the baptized [understand, *regenerate*] there remains concupiscence, or an incentive to sin. . . . This concupiscence, which the apostle sometimes calls sin, the holy Synod declares that the Catholic Church has never understood it to be called sin, as being truly and properly sin in those born again, but because it is of sin, and inclines to sin."

But if the fifth decree of Trent is largely ambiguous, the

Roman Catechism, of equal authority, is more explicit, and Bellarmin still more so.*

The Romish theory therefore locates the source of sin in Adam's unfallen nature. After the loss of the supernatural gift, he falls to the lower neutral level of his created state, and the struggle between the bodily appetites and the norms of reason naturally results in sin.

The similarity to Aristotle is that Adam was created neither sinful nor holy, but neutral. Maybe this is worse than Aristotle, for Adam's neutrality seems to offer no hope of achieving sinlessness; rather it seems that the body must inevitably overcome the mind.

The Reformed or Augustinian doctrine is that man was created righteous. The body had no downward propensities. No added supernatural gift was necessary to produce a harmony between body and spirit. Sin does not begin in the body—this is a remnant of Manichaeism—but in the mind. The result is total depravity, and the "concupiscence" even in the regenerate is truly and properly sin, as the apostle says.

But once again the discussion has leaped too far ahead. And again before the fall is discussed, it is necessary to explain federal headship, and before that, the covenant of works.

Genesis 2:17	But of the tree of the knowledge of good and evil, thou shalt not eat of it: for in the day that thou eatest thereof thou shalt surely die.
Luke 10:28	And he said unto him, Thou hast answered right: this do and thou shalt live.
Romans 2:6-8	Who will render to every man according to his deeds: To them who by patient continu-

---

*Compare W.G.T. Shedd, *History of Doctrine*, II, pp. 140 ff.

ance in well doing seek for glory and honour and immortality, eternal life: but unto them that are contentious, and do not obey the truth, but obey unrighteousness, indignation and wrath,

Romans 6:23   For the wages of sin is death; but the gift of God is eternal life through Jesus Christ our Lord.

Romans 10:5   For Moses describeth the righteousness which is of the law, That the man which doeth those things shall live by them.

Galatians 3:10   For as many as are of the works of the law are under the curse: for it is written, Cursed is every one that continueth not in all things which are written in the book of the law to do them.

Revelation 20:12   And I saw the dead, small and great, stand before God; and the books were opened: and another book was opened, which is the book of life: and the dead were judged out of those things which were written in the books, according to their works.

The idea of a covenant permeates Scripture, indeed the Bible itself is divided into two parts, called the Old Covenant and the New Covenant. The Children's Catechism defines covenant as an agreement between two or more persons. This does not require the equality of the parties. A victorious army can dictate the terms of peace to its defeated enemy. A father can lay down conditions in his will that bind his son. God laid down conditions for Adam's obedience. Being perfectly righteous at that time Adam certainly acquiesced without hesitation. But even though a defeated nation may hem and haw,

Clemenceau commands, "Signez!" and a covenant is made.

The covenant of works with Adam required him not to eat the fruit of a particular tree. Stated generally, the covenant required perfect obedience. The result of perfect obedience was to have been eternal life. As a general principle of divine justice this covenant is still in effect. As Romans 2:6-8 says, God will give eternal life to anyone who by patient good works seeks glory, honour, and incorruption. But while this covenant is still the standard of divine justice, it is inapplicable because there is no one that seeketh after God, all have sinned, and there is none that doeth good, no not one.

J.J. Van Oosterzee (*Christian Dogmatics,* Vol. I, p. 381) in rather peremptory phraseology rejects the idea of a covenant of works. He says, "There is not, however, the slightest ground for conceiving here of a properly so-called *covenant* made by God with all mankind in Adam, in which eternal life, as the reward of the work of obedience, was the promise, and the tree of life was the sign and seal (Coccejus). The exegetical grounds for this view in Hosea 6:7 are absolutely insufficient and its dogmatic value has not the slightest importance. Scripture does not teach that God has made a contract with man, but only that he designs to lead him, plainly by a moral road, to greater happiness."

How Van Oosterzee can defend the assertion, "its dogmatic value has not the slightest importance," is hard to guess. If the Bible does in fact teach a covenant of works, it must have some dogmatic importance. In fact the relation between the covenant of works and other parts of the plan of redemption will, as we proceed, become clear enough.

As for Hosea 6:7 one may translate it either, "But they like men have transgressed the covenant;" or, "they like Adam have transgressed the covenant." The first of these translations makes mediocre sense at best. Is it a very strong condemnation to say that they as well as other men have transgressed? The second translation is more pointed. It can be paraphrased as, they are not like ordinary sinners, they are worse, even similar to Adam in his first sin. With this translation the idea of a covenant with Adam is explicit.

However, the doctrine of a covenant of works does not depend on this isolated expression in Hosea. If a covenant is an agreement between two or more persons, the only factor not explicitly mentioned in Genesis is Adam's statement, "I agree." Now, if indeed Adam did not agree, there might be some reason for denying the existence of a covenant. But, since Adam had been created righteous, since further God and Adam, in Genesis 2:19, conversed as friends, and since the fact of this friendship is emphasized by the contrast of Adam's changed behavior in hiding from God in Genesis 3:8-10, it cannot be imagined that Adam had not agreed with the terms set down in Genesis 1:29 and 2:15 ff.

Further to support the idea of a covenant of works, it may be noted that the *threat* of death shows that death was not a natural end of life. The threat is good evidence that there was a covenant.

There is an understanding or interpretation of the particular test that throws light on some disturbing passages in the later Scriptures. Suppose God had commanded Adam not to murder Eve. God no doubt prohibited murder, for Cain seems to have known this law and trembled at its penalty. Presumably God gave all the Ten Commandments to Adam, either before the fall or immediately after. But the test of the covenant of works was the fruit of the tree and not the murder of Eve. Had it been the latter, Adam might have obeyed God simply because Eve was so beautiful. Obedience then would have followed upon mixed motives. But in the case of the fruit, whatever beauty it had was no sufficient motive for disobe-

dience; and the only motive for obedience was the bare desire
to obey God. Morality therefore is based on God's sovereignty.
His command alone makes an action right or wrong.

This explains some passages in I Samuel and elsewhere
that greatly disturb the modern mind. After the Philistines had
captured the Ark of the Lord, he discomfited them with rats
and bubonic plague. Therefore they sent the Ark back to the
Israelites. When the cows took the Ark to Bethshemesh, the
people of that place rejoiced greatly. They sacrificed the cows
as a burnt offering unto Jehovah. Yet, in spite of such joy and
thanksgiving, the Lord smote the men of Bethshemesh because
they had looked into the Ark. In fact the Lord killed 50,070
Israelites. Better known is the punishment of Uzzah in II
Samuel 6:7. The modern mind is disturbed by these severities
because it has an unbiblical concept of God and a false understanding of morality. Even Christians are contaminated with
these popular secular views. The Christian position is that
morality and righteousness are based on the sovereign commands of a sovereign God. An action is wrong simply because
God forbids it. Where there is no law, there is no sin to impute.
Had God given Adam no commands, Adam would have been
as free as the animals. They cannot sin; but Adam could and
did.

There was therefore a covenant of works.

10. Adam and the Fall: Federal Headship

If Adam had fulfilled the terms of the covenant, not only
he himself, but all his posterity also would have benefited. As it
turned out, we must be more interested in the result of his
disobedience. The two cases are in principle the same: His act,
good or bad, would determine the moral position of his de-

scendants. Though Genesis does not explain it at length, Adam's disobedience was not merely his personal and private sin. Even if this depraved nature was transmitted to his children by inheritance, this is not the full meaning of the fall because it is not the full meaning of Adam's relation to his posterity. The great passage on the subject is Romans 5:12-21: "Wherefore, as by one man sin entered the world, and by the sin death, and so death came upon all men because all sinned. . . . by the transgression of the one, the many died. . . . the judgment came from one to condemnation . . . by the transgression of the one; death reigned by the one. . . . So then as by one transgression the judgment came to all men to condemnation. . . . for as by one man's disobedience the many were constituted sinners, so also through the obedience of the one, the many shall be constituted righteous."

The student should now study Charles Hodge's superb *Commentary on Romans* for an exhaustive explanation of these verses. In fact all systematic theology presupposes preparatory exegesis. Ideally the student has covered most of the Bible in his exegesis courses, and now he is systematizing what he has previously learned. That is why theology text books, more advanced than this one, are often entitled, Systematic Theology.

So far as Romans 5:12-21 goes, there are three main interpretations. Each is learnedly, though sometimes perversely defended. The test of these interpretations, however, is simple. Only a person completely insane could deny that Paul in this passage constructs an analogy between Adam and Christ. Therefore any interpretation that ruins the analogy, that is, an interpretation that cannot be carried through with respect to both Adam and Christ, must be wrong.

The Pelagian interpretation is the worst of the three. Pelagius believed that Adam's sin had no effect on his posterity except that it furnished a bad example. Man has free will and he is able to obey the law of God perfectly. If a man uses his free will to obey sufficiently, inspired as he may be by Christ's example, he has earned his salvation.

This view does indeed preserve an analogy. But it is not Paul's analogy. Pelagius was consistent. We are sinners because of our own voluntary transgressions, and we achieve righteousness by our own good works. The analogy is complete; but both parts are false.

The first part is false because the Biblical text says that the many were made sinners by the one act of the one man; and it also says that many shall be made righteous, not by any alleged free will and obedience, but by the obedience of one man, Jesus. Note how Paul emphasizes the idea of the *one* act and the *one* person.

It may also be noted that Pelagius cannot explain the death of infants. On his theory they are born, if not righteous, at least neutral and not sinners, and therefore not deserving the penalty of death. Paul explains that infants die, even if they have not committed a voluntary sin after the similitude of Adam's first transgression. They are sinners by imputation.

The second view can be called either Romish or Arminian, or, sometimes, semi-pelagian. This theory holds that Adam's sin was not merely a bad example. By it his physical and mental constitution became depraved, and his natural posterity naturally inherited this depravity, and this depravity is the cause of death, even of infant deaths.

One point against this interpretation is the fact that the words "all sinned" in Romans 5:12 cannot be translated "all became corrupt." Paul says, "all sinned." The verb is not even a perfect tense, which could be translated "all have sinned and continue to be sinners." Normally the aorist tense refers to a single event in past time and here it refers to the one sin of the one man. How the one sin of Adam can justify the assertion that all sinned in that one act will be explained in a moment; but the verse cannot mean "all became corrupt."

Furthermore, this Romish-Arminian view destroys the analogy. Like the Pelagian view it also states an analogy. But the problem is not to invent some analogy or other; what is required is to preserve Paul's analogy and see that it is consistent with everything Paul teaches elsewhere. Now the Romish view is that though the depraved nature is not really sin, the sins that follow make us guilty of the death penalty. Similarly, infused grace results in those good works by which we merit salvation. But the New Testament is clear that the ground of our acquittal is no subjective state of ours, but the finished work and merit of Christ. The Arminians may not be so wrong on this point as the Romanists, for they profess to believe justification by faith. Nevertheless they tend to view our subjective believing as the basis of justification, and thereby at least to obscure and misunderstand Christ's merit.

Then, finally, the Biblical material shows that depravity is not the cause of death. Depravity is a part of death itself. Scripture uses the term *death* both for physical death and for spiritual death. Both together are the penalty for sin. God told Adam in Genesis 2:17, "In the day that thou eatest thereof thou shalt surely die." And die that day he did. About 900 years later he died physically. But this was only one part of the penalty for sin. The more immediate penalty was the depraving of his constitution. Therefore since depravity is a part of the penalty, it cannot be the cause of the penalty, as this view holds.

The third interpretation must therefore be correct. Adam was not only the natural head of the race, but God also chose him to be its representative. It was the race and not Adam alone that was on probation. If he sinned, then all sinned. Had he passed his probation, his children would have been sinless.

This view is sketchily given in Genesis. First, the penalty for disobedience descends to Adam's posterity (Genesis 3:15-16). Apparently also the righteousness established by probation, and its consequent freedom from death, would likewise have been transmitted. Note that the command to propagate the race comes before the fall. Adam and Eve would have had children. But they fell, and God drove them out of the garden lest they eat of the tree of life and live forever. This implies that the children, had there been no fall, would have had access to the tree of life. Hence the penalty descends, as the reward would have descended.

But what is so sketchily given in Genesis is fully explained in a paragraph not fully quoted a page or two ago:

Romans 5:17-19:   For if by one man's offense death reigned by one; much more they which receive abundance of grace and of the gift of righteousness shall reign in the life by one, Jesus Christ. Therefore as by the offense of one judgment came upon all men to condemnation; even so by the righteousness of one the free gift came upon all men unto justification of life. For as by one man's disobedience many were made sinners, so by the obedience of one shall many be made righteous.

The emphasis on the one man is overwhelming. By one man's offense, death reigned by the one. For the moment, omit the references to the one man Christ. By one transgression condemnation came upon all men. Through the disobedience of the one man, the many were made sinners.

If, now, Adam were not the representative of us all, and if

his first sin were not ours, then Paul could not have so stressed the one sin and ignored Adam's later sins. These later sins were also bad examples; if they did not initiate, they at least increased Adam's depravity. And why was not Eve's sin mentioned? Was it not also a bad example? Did it not deprave her? How then is the sin, depravity, and death of her posterity referred to Adam and not to Eve? The only answer can be that God chose Adam and not Eve to be our representative and to act in our stead.

The conclusion therefore is that Adam was the federal head or legal representative of his natural posterity. And when he sinned that one time, we all sinned.

11. Immediate Imputation

The federal headship of Adam may not seem germane to a descriptive psychology of human nature. As an office or function it does not even describe Adam's nature. But without it there is no understanding of the later generations—Cain, Lamech, Paul, and Alexander the coppersmith. Much of this material has already been touched upon, so that a reminder, some implications, and a small addition will be sufficient here. The small addition will be a defense of the consistency of immediate imputation with the philosophy of Realism, a consistency which Hodge denies.

In the discussion on traducianism it was necessary to anticipate the doctrine of immediate imputation. The essential point was there made clear: Depravity is a part of the penalty for sin, therefore the guilt logically precedes. The question is, on what ground does God hold us, Adam's posterity, guilty? The Biblical doctrine is that God imputes Adam's guilt to us immediately; that is, without an intermediary step. The word *immediately* here does not refer to time. One might say that God imputed Adam's guilt to us the very moment that Adam sinned. This could well be true, though it is more accurate to say that God imputed this guilt from all eternity. Clearly the doctrine of immediate imputation does not focus on time, as the contemporary usage of the word might suggest: The question is as stated above: Does God impute guilt because of our inherited depravity, or does he impute it without this as a means? The Biblical reason for the doctrine of immediate imputation is that depravity is a part of the penalty the guilt entails. We are not guilty because we are depraved; we are depraved because we are guilty.

Of course we are also guilty of our own voluntary transgressions here and now. This, however, is irrelevant to the present matter. The present matter is our relation to Adam's first sin.

The Westminster Confession uses a very carefully phrased paragraph to distinguish between inherited depravity and imputed guilt. It is so carefully yet so naturally worded that most readers probably fail to see the implications. The confessional statement is: "They being the root of all mankind, the guilt of this sin was imputed, and the same death in sin and corrupted nature conveyed to all their posterity descending from them by ordinary generation" (VI, 3). Note: the guilt was *imputed;* the corruption was *conveyed.*

None of this, to return to a previous point, conflicts with traducianism or realism. If there have been some theologians who asserted the preexistence of all souls, and somehow identify Adam's sin in a previous existence with a sin of ours in a previous existence, we agree that Plato taught preexistence and reincarnation. But he never identified Socrates with the Idea Man or with any other individual man. Hence realism cannot be rejected on the ground that Plato held both to realism and to preexistence. The former does not necessitate the latter.

It might then be asserted that realism is faulty because it cannot explain the relation of Adam's sin to our guilt. The obvious answer is that realism has no obligation to do so. The mere fact that genera and species are real, existing objects of thought is not very closely related to the problem of original sin. The fact that rosaceae is a genus has little to do with sending long stemmed roses to a lovely young lady. After all, neither does the doctrine of the Trinity explain the doctrine of original sin.

Hodge (*Systematic Theology* II, p. 217) admits that President Edwards' theory of original sin "is not exactly the old realistic theory." Indeed it is not. Edwards was not a realist at all. He was an empiricist, deeply influenced by Locke and Berkeley. Hence objections to Edwards damage neither realism nor traducianism. But Hodge wants to convict realism, even apart from Edwards. He writes (p.221) "The realistic doctrine . . . makes the numerical sameness of substance the essence of identity. Every genus or species of plants or animals is one because all the individuals of those genera and species are partakers of one and the same substance. In every species there is but one substance of which the individuals are the modes of manifestations." From this he infers that realism must identify the individual Adam with the individuals Peter and Paul.

But the difficulty, and of course there are others also, lies in the word *substance*. This is the word that causes difficulty in the doctrine of the Trinity. Since *substance* is Latin, and since it was given a different meaning from its Greek cognate *hypostasis,* one wants to know what Hodge means by it. If we use medieval Latin, we would not say that "in every species there is but one substance." We would say, "every species is one substance." Taking this back to Aristotle, this means that every species has a fixed *definition*. Plato would have said that the individuals *participate* in the Idea. In this way an individual could be called a mode of the Idea's or definition's manifestation. But this is far from identifying one mode of manifestation with another mode. That is, this is far from identifying the individual Adam with the individual Peter or Paul.

It is also far from identifying Adam with the species *homo sapiens*. A late Neoplatonist, Porphyry (c. 275), got his name attached to the phrase "a tree of Porphyry." This is a dichotomous scheme of classification. For example, Living Being is divided into immortal and mortal; mortal is divided into rational and irrational; irrational is divided into plant and animal. Now, then, this individual dachshund, Zephi, is a "manifestation" of the essence, definition, or reality *Dachshund*. He also participates in the essence or definition of *Dog;* and of *Animal.*

If anyone should suspect that Porphyry in the third century of our era cannot be trusted as a representative of Plato six centuries earlier, we may note that Plato's dialogue *Sophist* begins with a playful illustration of a "tree of Porphyry" in defining an angler. It eventually discusses the highest Ideas of Being, Same, Other, Rest and Motion; and concludes with another tree of Porphyry defining the Sophist. The dialogue *Parmenides* is too intricate to discuss here.

But even if Adam and Peter are "lowest species," they are not identical either with each other or with the higher species *homo*. Someone may now object that all this is too pagan. What has Athens to do with Jerusalem? This is the device of escapism. It evinces a disinclination to serious study. Yet a theologian may and ought to translate this material into more Biblical terminology. So we say, God knows, has the idea of, defines man, Adam, and Peter. God's knowledge is clear and distinct. He does not confuse one definition with another; he does not confuse Adam with Peter, or either one with the definition of man.

The conclusion then is that immediate imputation is a doctrine very obviously exegeted from Scripture; that realism, though not so quickly inferred by the average Bible reader, nevertheless underlies the Scriptural theory of truth and the presence of so-called abstract terms such as justification, and has further evidence in the pattern of the tabernacle; and finally that at the very least realism does not conflict with immediate imputation.

12. Total Depravity

Unlike the previous defense of the consistency of realism and immediate imputation, a subject that seems and is philosophical, because of which people with few logical proclivities fail to appreciate its Biblical importance, the doctrine of total depravity is of necessity more descriptive and more obviously Biblical. This doctrine has to do with the effects of sin in the history of the human race. Some of these effects are the actions of God; but more particularly they are the actions of Adam, Noah and his contemporaries, the sins of Israel, and our own. But not merely the actions: behind them is the depraved nature which engenders them.

Yet though the following is more temporally conditioned than the preceding, it is still mainly doctrinal. There are two reasons. First, the following is basically doctrinal because bare events are bare unless explained and explanation is doctrine. Then second, in Christianity history is itself doctrine. Although without the doctrinal explanation we would have no real understanding of the events, yet Christianity cannot be true unless the events actually occurred. The exodus from Egypt may not be so important as the death of Christ, but it is as essential to Christianity as the doctrine of the Atonement is. An explanation of an event—Christ died for our sins—is no explanation at all if the event did not occur.

So then, the first point in this section refers to a single historical event: Adam ate the forbidden fruit.

"Of man's first disobedience and the fruit of that
      forbidden tree,
Whose mortal taste brought death into the world and all
      our woe,
. . . . . .
Sing, heavenly Muse."

But the song is lugubrious, "for in the day that thou eatest thereof, thou shalt surely die."

Our discussion previously mentioned that this threat may seem not to have been fulfilled, for Adam lived several centuries after his initial disobedience. What this indicates, as explained above, is that *death* in the Scriptures does not primarily mean physical death. It means spiritual death, and this spiritual death brought us all our woe.

The first question now is, What became of the image of God when Adam fell? The Romish position that he fell to a level of neutrality was discussed earlier. The Bible and the Reformed position place him much lower. If he were neutral, there would have been the possibility of his regaining perfect righteousness by his own exertions. Such was Pelagius' dependence on free will. Further, if Adam had merely lost his original righteousness, the penalty God threatened to execute would have been inappropriate. Since the penalty was more severe than it seems to an uninstructed American pagan, one must ask, What happened to the image? Was it annihilated? Did man cease to be God's image?

The answer, as any partly educated Christian realizes, is,

No. Before the more fundamental reasons are considered, a particular application, and one of political importance today, is given in Genesis 9:6. The text says, "Whoso sheddeth man's blood, by man shall his blood be shed; for in the image of God made he man." The authority for capital punishment in the event of murder is based on the fact that the victim was the image of God. Naturally the secularists oppose capital punishment for murderers because they want to murder millions of unborn babies. This very practical consideration should stimulate in the untheological and unphilosophical Christian some respect for the more abstruse reasonings. To such we now return.

No; man did not cease to be God's image. Paradoxical though it may seem, man could not be a sinner at all, even now, if he were not still God's image. Sinning presupposes rationality and voluntary decision. Animals cannot sin. Sin therefore requires God's image because man is responsible for his sins. If there were no responsibility, there could be nothing properly called sin. Sin is an offense against God, and God calls us to account. If we were not answerable to God, repentance would be useless, indeed impossible nonsense. Reprobation and hell would also be impossible; for God has made responsibility a function of knowledge.

The same idea can be put another way. Whatever the fall did to man, it did not reduce him to the status of an irrational animal. Man is still man after the fall. He is still a person. He is still rational. To be sure, he acts irrationally. Yet his life is not one of instinct as is the case with animals. Sin does not eradicate the image; but it certainly causes a malfunctioning.

Theologians sometimes discuss, or more usually barely mention, the *noetic* effect of sin; and their remarks are often vague and hard to understand. Yet it should not be difficult to specify such noetic effects, that is, the effects of sin on the mind and rationality. The effect on the mind is not ignorance as such, for Adam was extensively ignorant before the fall. Not only was he ignorant of botany and calculus, he was ignorant of nearly all Biblical theology. The coming of a redeemer was revealed only after the fall, naturally and even then in puzzling brevity. The intellectual difference between Adam before the fall and afterwards was that after it he made mistakes. Error, not ignorance, is the effect. Before the fall, no matter how extensive his ignorance of mathematics may have been, whatever arithmetic he actually used was correct. Today we make mistakes in addition when we try to balance our bank statements. That is to say, Arminians do not understand the Bible.

The effect should be and can be stated more generally. Before the fall Adam may have reasoned relatively little, but his syllogisms were all valid. Afterward he fell into fallacies. He began to deny the antecedent, assert the consequent, and use too many undistributed middles. Sin had no effect on logic. Logic is the form of God's thought and a valid syllogism is valid even if it is the devil himself who uses it. Similarly with invalid inferences: no matter how saintly the devout Christian, his sanctification never makes an invalid inference valid. It is the sinner, not the logic, that is mistaken. Biologically he is still a rational species, but his mind has blundered. He does not always blunder in his inferences; the image is distorted, but not eradicated.

There is another type of error that man has fallen into. Not only are his inferences sometimes invalid: He often chooses false premises. Since this is rather obvious, its mention so far as formal logic is concerned should be sufficient. But there is one type of premise that requires special mention.

Questions of morality, in the more ordinary sense of the word (for a mistake in arithmetic is itself immoral, and that is why Arminianism was mentioned two paragraphs ago) are often divorced from discussions of logic, rationality, and even theology. Have we not all heard evangelists declaring that the unregenerate are not recalcitrant because of any theological difficulty: the trouble is moral.

A Nazarene professor once preached a sermon in Chicago on Christ's conversation with the woman at the well. She was not a woman of impeccable morality. When Christ reminded her that she was not married to the man she was living with, the woman, so the Nazarene professor declared, tried to side-step the issue of morality by asking a theological question on which the Jews and the Samaritans differed. But, said the professor, Christ could not be distracted, and he kept on pressing the matter of morality. Apparently the theological professor had never read the fourth chapter of John's Gospel. Christ very explicitly, even emphatically, gave the theological answer. There is not another word about morality or sin in the remainder of the conversation. In the preceding chapter Jesus had told the very pious Nicodemus, "Ye must be born again." To the woman he said, "God is spirit and they that worship him must worship him in spirit and in truth." Too bad: Poor Jesus got his two answers twisted around.

Yet even moral judgments are a species of judgment and are thus subsumed under general intellectual activity. One result of the fall, then, is the occurrence of incorrect evaluations by means of erroneous thinking. Adam thought, incorrectly, that it would be better to join Eve in her sin than to obey God and be separated from her. So without being deceived he ate the forbidden fruit. The external act followed upon the thought. "Out of the heart proceed evil thoughts." Commonly immorality is considered to consist in overt actions; the Bible shows its origin in thinking.

The topic of the noetic effects of sin, and the identification of God's image in man as reason or intellect, preserves the unity of man's person and saves theologians from splitting the image into schizophrenic parts. It accords with all that the Scripture says about sin and salvation.

Yet too many people in the pews, steeped in contemporary anti-intellectualism, and regarding all religion as essentially emotional, conclude that the noetic effects of sin is a subject too abstruse and philosophical, while on the other hand too many people who do not sit in the pews, the abortionists, the homosexuals, and assorted criminals, condemn Christianity as being too strict, bigoted, and any other unpleasant terms one can think of. The former group will be less than enthusiastic about any further emphasis on thinking, while the latter group will go their wicked way, hating and despising the Bible's characterization of prevalent sins.

In case some elementary students are unaware of it, and some secular professors too, one must inform them that the doctrine of total depravity does not mean that everyone is as sinful as it is possible to be. The word *total* in English can be used either extensively or intensively. The intensive or connotative idea is that man is so corrupt that his every act is as heinous an any act can be. The extensive or denotative sense is that all his thought, faculties, and activities, all of them, are to some degree or other affected by sin. In his totality he is indeed heading in the wrong direction, but only a few persons have actually descended to the lowest depths of their destination.

The doctrine of total depravity is essential to the theology of grace. If even one action, part, function or factor in man were free from the effects of sin, a sinner might expect that his salvation would depend, at least in part, on his own inherent goodness. Salvation might require the grace of God, but man's own goodness would also be requisite and effective. It cannot be emphasized too strongly that Christianity is a unified, logical system of doctrine and that various parts of theology which seem so disconnected are in fact absolutely essential to each other. A denial of total depravity is also a denial of salvation by Christ.

That the Scriptures definitely teach total depravity and base it on the noetic effects of sin, can easily be documented.

Genesis 6:5	And God saw that . . . every imagination of the thoughts of [man's] heart was only evil continually.
Job 14:4	Who can bring a clean thing out of an unclean? Not one.
Jeremiah 17:9	The heart is deceitful above all things and desperately wicked.
Matthew 15:19	Out of the heart proceed evil thoughts, murders, adulteries, . . . blasphemies.

And Romans 3:9-18, which we shall refrain from quoting.

These verses and dozens more, all of which, at least in their totality, rather definitely teach that sin affects every part of human nature, so that even the ploughing of the wicked is sin, are sufficient to justify the omission of a catalogue of actual sins. The sins themselves are of tremendous importance, but descriptive psychology could become very boring in describing them all. Some one or two could be analyzed for the benefit of a person today similarly tempted; but why here? One might begin with Cain, proceed to the utter wickedness of Noah's generation, repeat the story of Sodom, of Ahab, and of Judas. Perhaps more convincing are the sins of Jacob, of David, and Peter's denial. But why not just read the Bible? Some of the anti-philosophic readers would soon be happy with brief generalities, that is, the doctrinal summations. The present one is that human nature is depraved in all its parts.

13. The Heart

In addition to the basic principles relative to man's nature, the discussion of which sounds too philosophical for daily devotions, the Scripture exhibits numerous subsidiary details. Well, obviously, it had to, if it was going to describe the conduct of several hundred, or in groups several millions of people. It recounts the popular rejoicings and complaints by the people of Israel relative to Moses' administration of the new nation. The captivity and the return to Jerusalem were group phenomena. The Pharisees and the Sadducees combined in one group to oppose Christ. And the Stoics and Epicureans on Mars Hill dispersed when Paul began to mention the resurrection.

But human psychology is better described in the actions of individuals. Noah persevered for years in opposition to the prevailing opinions. Gideon gave the appearance of acting stupidly; and Samson certainly acted stupidly. Job is a wonderful example of trust in God during severe adversity. David sinned. Daniel resisted pressure. Consider the dozens of individuals whose actions the New Testament portrays. Such individualities are material for novels. For theology psychological terms must be examined.

The Bible speaks of the spirit, the soul, the mind, the conscience, and in the New Testament even the flesh, the usages of all of which are worthy of study. But nowhere in the Bible, at least in the King James version, is the word *emotion* to be found. One does, however, frequently find the term *heart*. Laidlaw (p. 121) remarks that "This is the one least disputed in its meaning . . . it may be held to be common to all parts of the Bible in the same sense. It only concerns the modern reader to note what that sense is, and to distinguish it, in one or two

particulars, from the modern use of the word." This statement
may be barely true. The term may possibly be the least disputed
among scholars, though it is hard to prove it. It is not used in
the Bible only in one sense. And if its modern use in Laidlaw's
day differed in just one or two particulars, it is today widely
misunderstood with deleterious effects. Many preachers inter-
pret it to be the antithesis of intellect. A recurrent contrast is
that between the heart and the head. If the head as intellect is
not totally repudiated, it is degraded to minor importance.
William E. Hocking, who did so much to destroy evangelical
foreign missions some fifty years ago, though he does not deny
that there are intellectual factors in religion, declared that no
theoretical proposition is true apart from feeling. I suppose
that in order to be true, $2 + 2 = 4$ must cause palpitation of the
heart. And conversely, though he might possibly admit that
not all passion is religious, passion is so much the medium of
religion that whatever is of passion "tends to be" religious.
James Bissett Pratt, in his *The Religious Consciousness*
(p. 123) asserts, "Nor is the intellectual side of the process of
conversion to be neglected, though it is frankly the least notice-
able of the three [will, emotion, and thought]. In most cases it
seems to play but a negative part." These two men were scholars and by their training disposed to speak cautiously. Popular
evangelists do not always do so.

Sometimes a Christian will insist that Jonathan Edwards
wrote a *Treatise Concerning Religious Affections*. Since no
one can deny that Jonathan Edwards was moderately well
educated, his interest in the emotions, so they say, is strong
evidence in favor of an emotional religion. But it is doubtful
that these Christians ever read even the first few pages of that
treatise. In the 1808 edition, printed by Edward Bains, in
Leeds, on pages 10-13 Edwards defines what he means by
affections. True, on page 9 he says that "true religion in great

part consists in holy affections." Could it be that the great Puritan was anticipating W.E. Hocking and J.B. Pratt? Does doctrine, in Edwards' view, "play but a negative part"? Is emotion, feeling, passion the really important factor?

The point is that Edwards' word *affections* does not mean *emotions*. On page 10 we read, or we ought to read rather than decide what his views were without reading, "Here it may be inquired, What the affections of the mind are? I answer, The affections are no other than the more vigorous and sensible exercises of the inclination and will of the soul." Surely no one will reply, "Ah, *sensible!* Edwards is talking about sensation." Well, the great Puritan did not deny that we have sensations, but in the very next line he continues: "God has endued the soul with two principal faculties: The one, that by which it is capable of *perception* and speculation, or by which it discerns and judges of things, which is called [not sensation, but] the *understanding*. The other, that by which the soul is some way *inclined* with respect to the things it views or considers: or it is the faculty by which the soul beholds things . . . either as liking, disliking . . . approving or rejecting. This faculty is called . . . inclination, will . . . mind . . . often called the heart."

Since a few more lines from Edwards may incline a student's will or mind to read some of his works, the quotation will continue a bit further. "It is not the body, but the mind only, that is the proper seat of the affections. . . . Nor are the motions of the animal spirits, and fluids of the body, anything properly belonging to the *nature* of the affections; though they always *accompany* them . . . [and] are entirely distinct from the affections themselves, and no way essential to them. . . . As all the exercises of inclination and will are concerned either in approving . . . or disapproving . . . so the affections are of two sorts . . . cleaving [to something] or [being] averse from it." On the next page he uses the terms inclination, will, and heart as synonymous.

The Lutherans too, at least those who like the Missouri Synod have preserved their orthodoxy, pay little or no attention to the emotions. Even in this century their notable theologian, Pieper, in his *Christian Dogmatics* (p. 519) very briefly, but twice, states the Lutheran position that the image consists of intellect and will. There is no mention of emotions.

This emphasis on the will has almost totally disappeared from what passes as Christian preaching. Freudianism has replaced it with the emotions. Most pew-warmers do not realize that this emphasis is a very modern development. One can go back to the Westminster divines, to Calvin, to Aquinas, to Augustine, and will find that human nature is regularly divided into intellect and will. To mention another philosopher, not altogether at random, Malebranche in the late seventeenth century began the first numbered paragraph of his *Récherché de la Vérité* with the words, "The spirit of man, not being material or extended, is doubtless a simple substance, indivisible and without composition of parts; but nevertheless it is customary to distinguish in it two faculties, to wit, understanding and volition. . . ." Emotions in theology seem to be a twentieth century invention. This development naturally altered people's views on regeneration and sanctification.

Augustine may seem an exception. The reason, however, was that he wanted to find a replica of the Trinity in man's mental make-up. He gave several different analyses of human nature. The most frequently mentioned third part was memory; and indeed he defended the identity of persons in heaven on the basis of memory. He also inclined to assign to the will a superiority over the intellect. Even today someone might argue that no one can learn anything without paying attention, and attention is a voluntary action. But Augustine's desire to find traces of the Trinity in man no longer dominates, and memory can be classified as intellectual, as when we remember that $2 + 2 = 4$.

These historical notes have given us a little information on the position of the church through the ages, but they have not advanced the main issue, which is the Biblical meaning of the word *heart*. But another, though this time a very slight, diversion will prove most helpful. Prior to the quotations, it seems best to state the conclusion finally to be drawn. The purpose is not to force the Scriptural material into a preconceived mold, but rather to direct the student's attention to certain ideas in the material. A single verse can express several ideas, on several subjects; stating the conclusion first will avoid irrelevancies in the examination. The conclusion will be that the term *heart* denotes emotion about ten or at the very most fifteen percent of the time. It denotes the will maybe thirty percent of the time; and it very clearly means the intellect sixty or seventy percent. These figures are obviously approximate. The term *heart* in the Bible occurs more than a thousand times. In view of the present writer's preference for intellectualism as opposed to emotionalism, his critics can easily suspect that he has deliberately chosen to present the intellectual verses—even though some extreme emotionalists may deny there are any at all—and to omit or to decrease the proportion of those on emotion. The only defense the writer has against such accusations is to challenge the critic to study all 1168 (?) verses. Those students who are as little inclined as I am to exegete them all must take my word for it that I have deliberately included a greater number of the emotional verses than I thought necessary. Fifteen percent of the Old Testament citations, if I quote seventy-five, would be 11.5 verses; and I do not think that the clearly emotional verses amount to fifteen percent.

Genesis 6:5, 6 was a passage used to support the doctrine

of total depravity, but now attention is directed to the term *heart*: "every imagination of the thoughts of his [man's] heart was only evil continually. . . . and it repented the Lord . . . and grieved him at his heart." Notice that the heart has thoughts: It thinks. The text refers to the evil plans of the populace, excluding Noah. Even the word *imagination* does not designate emotion. Similarly the second verse refers to God's thoughts. Repentance is a change of mind, not an emotion; and though God is immutable and never changes his mind, the Bible frequently uses anthropopathisms as well as anthropomorphisms. Strange to say, while few Christians are disturbed by the latter, many are deceived by the former. I doubt that any textbook on Systematic Theology written by a Calvinist, a Lutheran, or a Roman Catholic attributes emotion to God. One of them—I can't remember which one at the moment—explains God's anger as his immutable and eternal will to punish sin. Conversely love. Probably many Systematic Theologies say the same thing.

Genesis 8:21 refers both to the heart of God and the heart of man. In both cases it refers chiefly to volition, though both cases indicate a previous intellectual judgment.

Genesis 17:17 refers to a thought or judgment which Abraham made on the basis of his opinions regarding physiology. Genesis 20:5, 6 both refer to the intellectual integrity of Abimilech's heart. He sure had emotions! But both verses concern his mistaken, though excusable, conclusion.

Genesis 24:45 describes the intellectual formulation of a plan of action. No emotion is implied at all. Genesis 27:41 has to do with Esau's plan to murder Jacob. True enough, Esau hated Jacob, and this was no doubt an emotion; but the *heart* is mentioned in connection with a decision on the time to commit the murder. It was pure intellection and not even volition.

Genesis 42:28 may be cited as a case of emotion, for fear is presumably an emotion. When Joseph's brothers on their return from Egypt found their money in their sacks, "their heart failed them." In Genesis 45:26 "Jacob's heart fainted, for he believed them not." The disbelief was an intellectual act, but the fainting was emotional.

Ten verses from Genesis have now been quoted; eight are rather clearly intellectual, while two are distinctly emotional.

Exodus has about twenty references to God's hardening Pharaoh's heart, or Pharaoh's hardening his own heart, or simply the hardening of his heart. Virtually all of them indicate a voluntary determination to retain the Israelites in slavery. Exodus 4:14 is rather clearly emotional, along with 35:21 and 36:2. On the intellectual side there are 35:34, 35. I hope this is a fairly accurate report on Exodus. Let it also be said that Leviticus 19:17 has to do with the emotions.

Suppose we now skip to I Samuel 1:8, 13; 2:1; 9:19; 14:7; 27:1; and 28:5. The first of these is clearly an emotion, and 1:13 has this emotional background though explicitly it is a prayer and therefore intellectual. Also emotional is 2:1, though it too is a prayer. The next three are intellectual and the last is the emotion of fear. There are in all, I believe, twenty-three occurrences of the term *heart* in First Samuel, and fourteen in Second Samuel. The latter's first case, 3:21, I would classify as intellectual, or perhaps volitional, but hardly emotional. Michal in 6:16 may have been emotional, but there had to be a normative judgment too. God's plan and David's knowledge, in 7:21, are equally intellectual, as 7:27 also is. Amnon's heart in 13:23 was about to be emotionally drunk, but 13:33 refers to a piece of misinformation.

However tedious this brief list has become, and whatever omissions are justifiable, the Psalms cannot be disregarded. I judge the term occurs about 130 times. Can we be satisfied with thirteen of them?

Psalm 4:4, 7 are "Commune with your own heart upon your bed and be still. . . . Thou hast put gladness in my heart." The latter verse may indicate some lesser degree of emotion, but the former definitely speaks of meditation, an intellectual process of thought when one is calm and not upset emotionally. How many Christians today, during a wakeful period about 2:00 a.m., meditate on a verse or two and try to understand its implications? Of course, there is some danger in this: The verse may become so interesting that you can't get back to sleep before 3:30.

Psalm 9:1 reads, "I will praise thee, O Lord, with my whole heart." The emotionalists will count this one in their favor, but acceptable praise cannot be devoid of correct theology. Psalm 10:11, 13 are, "He hath said in his heart, God hath forgotten . . . he will never see it. . . . [the wicked man] hath said in his heart Thou will not require it." This is obviously intellectual. To be sure the wicked man is making false statements, but they are nonetheless intellectual judgments. They are theological blunders. He is denying God's immutability and his omniscience, as well as his eternal decree to punish the wicked.

Psalm 12:2 says, "With flattering lips and with a double heart they do speak," and thus describes insincerity. The man is practicing deceit. One of his hearts contains his real opinions, while his other heart pronounces opposite judgments.

Psalm 19 is a great Psalm, and 19:4 is a great verse. After several references to the law and statutes of God, his judgments and testimony, all of which are intellectual truth, the Psalmist concludes, "Let the words of my mouth and the meditations of my heart be acceptable in thy sight, O Lord, my strength and my redeemer." Here the Psalmist prays to God that his thoughts on the Atonement may be true. And not only his thoughts: also his words when he preaches publicly. We cannot assume that his words were spoken to nobody.

Psalm 24:4 speaks of clean hands and a pure heart. This seems best classified as volitional, yet holy actions presuppose holy thinking.

Psalm 36:1, 10 first pictures the Psalmist as concluding in his heart that the wicked do not fear God. This is of course an intellectual judgment. Then second the Psalmist prays that God continue his loving-kindness to them that know thee, and thy righteousness to the upright in heart. This tenth verse speaks of knowledge and then of righteousness. The latter is probably a volitional reference, but it is made against an intellectual background. At any rate there is nothing emotional here.

"The law of his God is in his heart" (Psalm 37: 31) is clearly intellectual. The previous verse mentioned wisdom and judgment, and the law is something that must be understood.

Look at 45:1, "My heart is inditing [overflows with; metaphorical for "is occupied with;" *indite*: compose or write down] a good matter . . . my tongue is the pen of a ready writer." The verse is completely intellectual, as is also Psalm 49:3, "wisdom; and the meditation of my heart shall be of understanding."

Just prior to this list from the Psalms a question was asked: Can we be satisfied with thirteen of them? Thirteen have now been given. If anyone prefers to skip the next eleven, he may do so; but two dozen impresses the writer more favorably than a baker's dozen. The aim is to leave no doubt but that the heart fundamentally means the intellect and surely not the emotions.

Psalm 53:1 reminds us of some present day intellectual boasting: "The fool hath said in his heart, there is no God." Intellection may be righteous or sinful; but in either case it is thinking and not emoting. Psalm 77:6 is again intellectual meditation; and 78:8 could be volitional; and 78:72 is both.

Psalm 84:5 is volitional; 86:11, 12 are partly intellectual,

"Teach me thy way, O Lord," and partly volitional, "I will praise thee, O Lord, with my whole heart." Psalm 95:8, 10 are rather clearly volitional.

But Psalm 119 is intellectual throughout. Verse 7 says, "I will praise thee with uprightness of heart when I shall have learned thy righteous judgments." Verse 11 is the well known statement, "Thy word I have hid in my heart." Here the Psalmist tells us that he had memorized much of the Scripture that had already been written at that time. Of course it is a recommendation to us also not to be intellectually lazy, but to learn the Scriptures by heart. You can't do that with your emotions. Verse 36 inclines the heart to God's testimonies, and verse 69 repeats the same general idea: "I will keep thy precepts with my whole heart." If the "keeping" is volitional, it presupposes, as was previously stated, an earlier process of learning those testimonies.

Now, without continuing to Proverbs 2:2, 10 (very clear), 3:1, 4:4 and to the remainder of the Old Testament, it seems that more than eleven verses have been added to the thirteen.

The conclusion is that the *heart* in the Old Testament* designates the intellect most of the time; it designates volition maybe one third of the time; it refers to the emotions maybe a bit more than ten percent of the time.

Therefore when someone in the pews hears the preacher contrasting the head and the heart, he will realize that the preacher either does not know or does not believe what the Bible says. That the gospel may be proclaimed in its purity and power, the churches should eliminate their Freudianism and other forms of contemporary psychology and return to God's

---

*Howard Marshall, *The Epistles of John* (Erdmanns, 1978), in footnote 5 on page 198 says, "In Hebrew thought the heart is tantamount to the conscience." Evidently he had not studied the 1,168 instances.

Word, to which nothing should be added and from which nothing should be subtracted.

14. A Philosophic Appendix

There are no doubt a few more psychological terms which could be discussed. For example, the term *flesh* in the New Testament does not always mean muscles and sinews. It often denotes the sinful proclivities of human nature. The term *spiritual* also as often refers to the results of the Holy Spirit's operations as it does to the soul. But these items do not raise problems equal in difficulty and importance with what has been discussed. A very different problem of tremendous difficulty will serve as a concluding appendix for anyone patient enough to read it.

Identifying the soul, spirit, or mind as the man himself—and this is what the preceding material has done—raises philosophic perplexities of the highest order. But let it be noted that any theory not identifying man with mind faces the same embarrassing dilemmas. The question is, What is the relation of body to soul? Even the behaviorists, who deny the existence of a soul, though they escape the one question, sink into a deeper quagmire.*

The question therefore is, How can an extended, inert lump of clay affect a non-spatial active spirit? Or conversely, How can a non-spatial spirit initiate or direct the motions of a physical body?

Tertullian tried to evade the embarrassments—though in his age they were not so keenly felt—by making the soul a fiery breath, an idea he probably accepted from Stoicism. Vigorous

---

*Compare G.H. Clark, *Behaviorism and Christianity* (Jefferson, Maryland: The Trinity Foundation, 1982).

Christian though he was, and precursor of the doctrine of the Trinity, he has the dubious honor of being a Christian materialist. I can think of only one other, an Englishman.

Augustine, more Neoplatonic than Stoic, realized that the spirit was not corporeal. By a theory of causation he argued that since causality always descends from the superior to the inferior, the body never affects the soul: the soul controls the body. Unfortunately this principle does not explain *how* the unextended can initiate or alter corporeal motions.

Sometimes Descartes is either praised or blamed for sharpening the antithesis. He held that God created two substances, material and spiritual. The soul is an unextended point in the pineal gland of the brain and there it can alter the direction of the animal spirits (as brandy is a *spirit*) and so control the body without changing the magnitude of the motion. Clearly this does not explain how a mathematical point can in any way alter physical motion. The usual idea is that one body has to bump another body.

Following Descartes several philosophers made serious efforts to solve the problem. What then is the relationship between the inert clay from which God formed Adam's body and the active, even turbulent breath that he breathed into Adam's nostrils? Though most evangelical theologians have something to say on the matter, H.B. Smith, *System of Christian Theology* (New York, 1864, pp. 164-165) has perhaps the clearest and most concise statement of the several positions. I shall not quote verbatim but be content to follow his order and extend his description.

The first theory mentioned is materialism, or, since no one any longer holds to classical materialism, behaviorism, according to which what we call conscious life is precisely the functioning of bodily parts. Today even some who profess to be Christian accept this theory. They picture a human being as a complex electric circuit on a sign that flashes an advertisement. Long ago Plato clearly stated how this is in utter conflict with Christianity. His example, instead of being an electric circuit, was that of a lyre, whose functioning, illustrative of the soul, is the music; but after the lyre is broken, there can be no more music. Thus the soul does not outlive the body.

Materialism can be called a monistic theory. The second is also monistic, but also quite the opposite of the first. Instead of denying the soul, it denies the matter. The view can be called idealism. The good Bishop Berkeley was an idealist. This is a more reasonable theory than the first one, for (1) it is hard to see how matter can become thought, while (2) it is relatively easy to see how sensory perceptions, which are elements of consciousness, could be mistakenly assigned unconscious causes. Later Hegel and his disciples produced an idealism rather different from Berkeley's and pretty well held the field until defeated in World War I.

If now idealism must be rejected, one must accept some kind of dualism. This presumably requires Descartes' two substances—whatever the term substance might mean. We do not necessarily have Descartes' pineal gland to explain their relationship. Malebranche in his *The Search for Truth* (1674) published a new tentative. Well, not entirely new. The medieval philosopher, the Moslem Al Gazali, denied physical causation and referred all events immediately to the will of God. Zwingli also seems to have suggested something similar in his emphasis on the sovereignty of God.* But Malebranche goes into detail.†

---

*Frank Hugh Foster, in a supplementary chapter to Samuel Macauley Jackson's *Huldreich Zwingli*, p. 379, quotes Zwingli's *Werke*, ed. by Schuler u. Schulthess, p. 85.

†Lévy-Bruhl gives a readable account in his *History of Modern Philosophy in France*, Open Court, 1924, pp. 38-76. But if the student can do nothing more, he should read the Preface to *La Récherché*.

First he attacks the confused notion of causality. Theologians use the term glibly, but they never define it. The Westminster Confession states that God's decree establishes secondary causes, but it gives no hint as to what they are or how they operate. The term *cause* is of course correlative with the term *effect*. If there be no effect, there could have been no cause. If there is a cause, the effect results necessarily. But no such relationship is found in sensory experience. If someone says that eating good food is the cause of nourishment, a touch of seasickness will disabuse his mind. Eating good food does not necessitate nourishment. The so-called cause can occur and the alleged effect fail. Hence the soul cannot cause a bodily motion. In fact there are no causes and effects in natural phenomena. This is rather interesting, for it means that Malebranche anticipated modern science in rejecting occult qualities and the like and in defining the scientific enterprise as a description of motions. Hume thus was not so original as he has often been thought to be. For that matter, Malebranche was not completely original, either; for Descartes understood that science could not discover God's purposes and that theological explanations must be replaced with mathematical equations.

Since no one can see the soul affecting the body, why does it seem so? Aside from the intellectual lethargy of the general public and its unquestioning acceptance of traditional ignorance, the worlds of space and mind, in the light of revelation, do have an understandable relationship. Malebranche's explanation of this is a theory called Occasionalism. God is the sole and indefeasibly effective cause of everything throughout the universe. He speaks and it is done. God produces mental events and physical events immediately. That is to say, when one sticks one's finger with a pin and experiences a pain, it is not the pin that produced the pain. God did.

There is another possibility. Leibniz did not favor the notion that God immediately causes every event. In a somewhat deistic fashion he held that God manufactured two clocks—body and soul—so perfectly adjusted to each other that when one strikes three (the three illustrating the pin prick) the other clock strikes three at the same moment (illustrating the pain). This theory is called pre-established harmony. God originally constructed the universe so that everything would dove-tail. Leibniz was not really so interested in the relation between bodies and souls as he was in the relationships among persons. The various human beings are like a number of musicians, each in a different room; but they each have a score before them, written by the same composer, for flute, violin, or bassoon as the case may be; then, oblivious to one another, at a creative signal all begin to play, and the 1812 overture of war, peace, and politics sounds forth.

Even though more deistic than Malebranche, Leibniz had one advantage over him. His problem is different. The Frenchman, as a disciple of Descartes, struggled with the relationship between spatial bodies and non-spatial souls. For Leibniz the elements were not bodies: they were monadic non-extended souls. A body is like a school of fish: We do not see the individual fishes below the surface; what we see is a long shape, deceptively continuous. He thus anticipated our contemporary view that apparently solid objects, not only human bodies, but pens and pencils, have no contiguous parts, but are ninety-nine percent empty space. This must suffice for now. Interested students must go to their university libraries or take a good course in physics.

But the discussion has not been so unbiblical and untheological as the uninitiated suppose. The more obvious religious consideration is that theologians write Systematic Theologies without a sufficient background. H.B. Smith, after his excellent outline of the several positions sums it all up by saying, "The simple facts are, however, . . . that they [soul and body] do interact." He gives no reason: It is true simply because he says so.

Now, Malebranche was a Roman Catholic and rather strongly so. His type of theology is anathema to Calvinists. But insofar as he defends some Augustinian positions, he can serve as a corrective to the anti-intellectualism of the present day, its existentialism, combined as it is with non-biblical psychology and sociology. For this reason I shall translate a few paragraphs of the powerful Préface to *La Récherché de la Vérité*, to the praise of the God of Truth.

> The spirit of man is by its nature placed between its Creator and bodily creatures. . . . But as the great elevation by which it is above all material things does not prevent it from being united to them . . . so the infinite distance between the sovereign Being and the human spirit does not prevent it from being immediately united to him in a most intimate manner. This latter union elevates it above all things; by that union it receives its life, its light, and all its felicity. . . . On the contrary, the union of the spirit with the body abases man infinitely, and it is now the principal cause of all our errors and all our miseries.

> I am not surprised that ordinary people or pagan philosophers only consider the soul in its relation and union with the body, without recognizing the relation and union it has with God; but I am surprised that Christian philosophers, who ought to prefer the spirit of God above the spirit of man, Moses above Aristotle, Augustine above some miserable commentator of a pagan philosopher, are

more interested in the soul as the form of the body than as made in the image and for the image of God . . . to whom it is immediately united. . . .

. . . Since the will of God regulates the nature of every thing, it is more the nature of the soul to be united to God by a knowledge of the truth and by the love of good, than to be united to the body, because it is certain . . . that God made our spirits in order to know him and to love him rather than to impose a form on the body. . . .

The sin of the first man so weakened the union of our spirit with God that . . . that union appears imaginary to those who blindly follow the judgments of sense and the urgings of passion.

On the contrary, it [the first sin] has so strengthened the union of our soul with our body that it seems to us that these two parts of ourselves are no more than a single substance; or, rather, it has so subjected us to our senses and our emotions that we are brought to believe that our body is the principal one of the two parts of which we are composed.
. . .

The soul, although united very strictly to the body, does not cease being united to God; and at the very time when it is receiving from its body those feelings, lively and confused, which its passions inspire in it, it is [also] receiving from the eternal truth which presides over its spirit the knowledge of its duty and its shortcomings. When the body deceives it, God undeceives it. . . .

. . . A man who judges everything by his senses, who always follows the movements of his passions, who perceives only what he senses . . . is in the most miserable state of spirit that he could be in; . . . But when a man judges things only by the pure ideas of the spirit, and carefully avoids the confused noise of the creatures, and when retiring into himself he hears his sovereign Maker, with his senses and passions silent, it is impossible for him to fall into error.

. . . but when the spirit turns from God and goes outside, when he interrogates only his body in seeking the truth, when he listens only to his senses, his imagination, and his passions, it is impossible for him to escape deception. . . .

The body fills the spirit with such a great number of sensations that it becomes incapable of knowing the least hidden of truths. . . . It is only by the attention of the spirit that any truth is discovered and any knowledge is gained; because indeed the attention of the spirit is nothing other than its return and conversion to God, who is our only Teacher . . . as St. Augustine says.

Scripture Index

Index

Mozart, 56
Mueller, John Theodore, 20-21;
 Works: Christian Dogmatics,
 20
Murder, 23, 61, 73

Natural law, 4
Nature, 58
Nephesh, 10, 37-39, 41
Neshamah, 37
New American Standard
 Version, 29
Nicene Council, 34
Nicodemus, 75
Nietzsche, Friedrich, 25
Noah, 71, 77-78, 83
Noetic effects of sin, 73-77

Obedience, 64
Observation, 23-24, 27; *see also*
 Empiricism
Occasionalism, 91
Oehler-Day, 37; *Works: Old*
 Testament Theology, 37
Old Testament, 8
Old Testament Theology
 (Oehler-Day), 37
Olshausen, 43
Omniscience, of God, 21
Onomatopoeia, 55
Oosterzee, J.J. Van, 60; *Works:*
 Christian Dogmatics, 60
Original sin, 44, 57, 69; *see also*
 Sin

Outlines of Theology (A.A.
 Hodge), 51
Owen, John, 44, 48; *Works:*
 Commentary on Hebrews, 44

Palmer, Ben W., 32; *Works:*
 "Hobbes, Holmes, and
 Hitler," 32
Parallelism, 39
Parmenides (Plato), 70
Pascal, Blaise, 21
Paul, 3, 10, 28, 63-64, 67, 69,
 70, 78
Pelagianism, 8, 43
Pelagius, 43, 63-64, 72
Pendulum, law of, 23
Perception, 26, 80, 90; *see also*
 Empiricism, Experience,
 Observation, Sensation
Peter, 10, 69-70, 77
Pharaoh, 84
Pharisees, 78
Philistines, 62
Philo, 5, 42
Philosophy, 2, 4-5, 15, 34
Philosophy of John Dewey, The
 (Schlipp), 27
Physics, 2, 4-5, 22-23, 29, 92;
 see also Science
Pieper, Francis, 20-21, 81;
 Works: Christian Dogmatics,
 20
Piltdown Man, 2-3; *see also*
 Evolution
Pinnock, Clark, 19

Plato, 4, 29, 34, 41, 49, 68, 70,
    90; *Works: Parmenides,* 7;
    Phaedo, 29; *Sophist,* 70
Platonism, 25
Plotinus, 15
Pneuma, 42
Pope, 13
Pope, Alexander, 15
Porphyry, 70
Pratt, James Bissett, 79-80;
    *Works: The Religious
    Consciousness,* 79
Pre-established harmony, 92
Preexistence, 68
Propositions, universal, 23
Psuche, 40, 42
Psychology, 4, 15, 42-44, 67,
    77-78, 87, 93
Punishment, 22, 32; capital, 73
Pythagoras, 31

Racism, 3
Rationalism, 25
Rationality, 6, 12, 18, 53, 55,
    73-75
Realism, 48-49, 67-69, 71
Reason, 16-17, 56-57, 58
Récherché de la Vérité
    (Malebranche), 81, 90-95
Recollection, 27
Redemption, 1, 43, 60
Regeneration, 13, 42-44, 56, 81
Reincarnation, 68
Religious liberty, 2
Repentance, 73, 83

Reprobation, 73
Responsibility, 22, 73
Resurrection, 16, 39, 78
Revelation, 11, 15, 33, 91
Righteousness, 8, 12-14, 16,
    20, 32, 55, 57, 59, 66, 72, 86
Roman Catechism, 58
Roman Catholic church, 8, 12,
    46, 56, 57, 64
Roos, M.F., 43
Rousseau, Jean-Jacques, 54
Ruach (spirit), 37-38
Ryle, Gilbert, 26-27

Sabbath, 52
Sadducees, 78
Saints, treasury of, 13
Salvation, 13, 17, 29, 53, 57,
    64-65, 76-77
Samson, 78
Sanctification, 44, 81
Saturn, 20
Schlipp, 27; *Works: The
    Philosophy of John Dewey,* 27
Science, 3-5, 20, 21, 25, 91
Scofield Bible, 39
Scofield, C.I., 40-42
Search for Truth, The (Nicolas
    Malebranche), 81, 90-95
Sensation, 16, 19, 22, 28, 35,
    80, 95; *see also* Empiricism
Sense, 94-95
Sensory experience, 19, 21, 23,
    91
Shedd, W.G.T., 34n., 48-50, 52,

The Crisis of Our Time

Historians have christened the thirteenth century the Age of Faith and termed the eighteenth century the Age of Reason. The twentieth century has been called many things: the Atomic Age, the Age of Inflation, the Age of the Tyrant, the Age of Aquarius. But it deserves one name more than the others: the Age of Irrationalism. Contemporary secular intellectuals are anti-intellectual. Contemporary philosophers are anti-philosophy. Contemporary theologians are anti-theology.

In past centuries secular philosophers have generally believed that knowledge is possible to man. Consequently they expended a great deal of thought and effort trying to justify knowledge. In the twentieth century, however, the optimism of the secular philosophers has all but disappeared. They despair of knowledge.

Like their secular counterparts, the great theologians and doctors of the church taught that knowledge is possible to man. Yet the theologians of the twentieth century have repudiated that belief. They also despair of knowledge. This radical skepticism has filtered down from the philosophers and theologians and penetrated our entire culture, from television to music to literature. *The Christian in the twentieth century is confronted with an overwhelming cultural consensus—sometimes stated explicitly, but most often implicitly: Man does not and cannot know anything truly.*

111

What does this have to do with Christianity? Simply this: If man can know nothing truly, man can truly know nothing. We cannot know that the Bible is the Word of God, that Christ died for the sins of his people, or that Christ is alive today at the right hand of the Father. Unless knowledge is possible, Christianity is nonsensical, for it claims to be knowledge. What is at stake in the twentieth century is not simply a single doctrine, such as the Virgin Birth, or the existence of hell, as important as those doctrines may be, but the whole of Christianity itself. If knowledge is not possible to man, it is worse than silly to argue points of doctrine—it is insane.

The irrationalism of the present age is so thorough-going and pervasive that even the Remnant—the segment of the professing church that remains faithful—has accepted much of it, frequently without even being aware of what it was accepting. In some circles this irrationalism has become synonymous with piety and humility, and those who oppose it are denounced as rationalists—as though to be logical were a sin. Our contemporary anti-theologians make a contradiction and call it a Mystery. The faithful ask for truth and are given Paradox. If any balk at swallowing the absurdities of the anti-theologians, they are frequently marked as heretics or schismatics who seek to act independently of God.

There is no greater threat facing the true Church of Christ at this moment than the irrationalism that now controls our entire culture. Totalitarianism, guilty of tens of millions of murders, including those of millions of Christians, is to be feared, but not nearly so much as the idea that we do not and cannot know the truth. Hedonism, the popular philosophy of America, is not to be feared so much as the belief that logic—that "mere human logic," to use the religious irrationalists' own phrase—is futile. The attacks on truth, on revelation, on the intellect, and on logic are renewed daily. But note well: The misologists—the haters of logic—use logic to demonstrate the futility of using logic. The anti-intellectuals construct intricate intellectual arguments to prove the insufficiency of the intellect. The anti-theologians use the revealed Word of God to show that there can be no revealed Word of God—or that if there could, it would remain impenetrable darkness and Mystery to our finite minds.

Nonsense Has Come

Is it any wonder that the world is grasping at straws—the straws of experientialism, mysticism and drugs? After all, if people are told that the Bible contains insoluble mysteries, then is not a flight into mysticism to be expected? On what grounds can it be condemned? Certainly not on logical grounds or Biblical grounds, if logic is futile and the Bible unintelligible. Moreover, if it cannot be condemned on logical or Biblical grounds, it cannot be condemned at all. If people are going to have a religion of the mysterious, they will not adopt Christianity: They will have a genuine mystery religion. "Those who call for Nonsense," C.S. Lewis once wrote, "will find that it comes." And that is precisely what has happened. The popularity of Eastern mysticism, of drugs, and of religious experience is the logical consequence of the irrationalism of the twentieth century. There can and will be no Christian revival—and no reconstruction of society—unless and until the irrationalism of the age is totally repudiated by Christians.

The Church Defenseless

Yet how shall they do it? The spokesmen for Christianity have been fatally infected with irrationalism. The seminaries, which annually train thousands of men to teach millions of

Christians, are the finishing schools of irrationalism, completing the job begun by the government schools and colleges. Some of the pulpits of the most conservative churches (we are not speaking of the apostate churches) are occupied by graduates of the anti-theological schools. These products of modern anti-theological education, when asked to give a reason for the hope that is in them, can generally respond with only the intellectual analogue of a shrug—a mumble about Mystery. They have not grasped—and therefore cannot teach those for whom they are responsible—the first truth: "And ye shall know the truth." Many, in fact, explicitly deny it, saying that, at best, we possess only "pointers" to the truth, or something "similar" to the truth, a mere analogy. Is the impotence of the Christian Church a puzzle? Is the fascination with pentecostalism and faith healing among members of conservative churches an enigma? Not when one understands the sort of studied nonsense that is purveyed in the name of God in the seminaries.

The Trinity Foundation

The creators of The Trinity Foundation firmly believe that theology is too important to be left to the licensed theologians —the graduates of the schools of theology. They have created The Trinity Foundation for the express purpose of teaching the faithful all that the Scriptures contain—not warmed over, baptized, secular philosophies. Each member of the board of directors of The Trinity Foundation has signed this oath: "I believe that the Bible alone and the Bible in its entirety is the Word of God and, therefore, inerrant in the autographs. I believe that the system of truth presented in the Bible is best summarized in the Westminster Confession of Faith. So help me God."

The ministry of The Trinity Foundation is the presentation of the system of truth taught in Scripture as clearly and as completely as possible. We do not regard obscurity as a virtue, nor confusion as a sign of spirituality. Confusion, like all error, is sin, and teaching that confusion is all that Christians can hope for is doubly sin.

The presentation of the truth of Scripture necessarily involves the rejection of error. The Foundation has exposed and will continue to expose the irrationalism of the twentieth century, whether its current spokesman be an existentialist philosopher or a professed Reformed theologian. We oppose anti-intellectualism, whether it be espoused by a neo-orthodox theologian or a fundamentalist evangelist. We reject misology, whether it be on the lips of a neo-evangelical or those of a Roman Catholic charismatic. To each error we bring the brilliant light of Scripture, proving all things, and holding fast to that which is true.

The Primacy of Theory

The ministry of The Trinity Foundation is not a "practical" ministry. If you are a pastor, we will not enlighten you on how to organize an ecumenical prayer meeting in your community or how to double church attendance in a year. If you are a homemaker, you will have to read elsewhere to find out how to become a total woman. If you are a businessman, we will not tell you how to develop a social conscience. The professing church is drowning in such "practical" advice.

The Trinity Foundation is unapologetically theoretical in its outlook, believing that theory without practice is dead, and that practice without theory is blind. The trouble with the professing church is not primarily in its practice, but in its theory. Christians do not know, and many do not even care to

know, the doctrines of Scripture. Doctrine is intellectual, and
Christians are generally anti-intellectual. Doctrine is ivory
tower philosophy, and they scorn ivory towers. The ivory tower,
however, is the control tower of a civilization. It is a fundamental, theoretical mistake of the practical men to think that they
can be merely practical, for practice is always the practice of
some theory. The relationship between theory and practice is
the relationship between cause and effect. If a person believes
correct theory, his practice will tend to be correct. The practice
of contemporary Christians is immoral because it is the
practice of false theories. It is a major theoretical mistake of the
practical men to think that they can ignore the ivory towers of
the philosophers and theologians as irrelevant to their lives.
Every action that the "practical" men take is governed by the
thinking that has occurred in some ivory tower—whether that
tower be the British Museum, the Academy, a home in Basel,
Switzerland, or a tent in Israel.

In Understanding Be Men

It is the first duty of the Christian to understand correct
theory—correct doctrine—and thereby implement correct
practice. This order—first theory, then practice—is both logical and Biblical. It is, for example, exhibited in Paul's epistle to
the Romans, in which he spends the first eleven chapters
expounding theory and the last five discussing practice. The
contemporary teachers of Christians have not only reversed
the order, they have inverted the Pauline emphasis on theory
and practice. The virtually complete failure of the teachers of
the professing church to instruct the faithful in correct doctrine
is the cause of the misconduct and cultural impotence of
Christians. The Church's lack of power is the result of its lack
of truth. The *Gospel* is the power of God, not religious

experience or personal relationship. The Church has no power because it has abandoned the Gospel, the good news, for a religion of experientialism. Twentieth century American Christians are children carried about by every wind of doctrine, not knowing what they believe, or even if they believe anything for certain.

The chief purpose of The Trinity Foundation is to counteract the irrationalism of the age and to expose the errors of the teachers of the church. Our emphasis—on the Bible as the sole source of truth, on the primacy of the intellect, on the supreme importance of correct doctrine, and on the necessity for systematic and logical thinking—is almost unique in Christendom. To the extent that the church survives—and she will survive and flourish—it will be because of her increasing acceptance of these basic ideas and their logical implications.

We believe that the Trinity Foundation is filling a vacuum in Christendom. We are saying that Christianity is intellectually defensible—that, in fact, it is the only intellectually defensible system of thought. We are saying that God has made the wisdom of this world—whether that wisdom be called science, religion, philosophy, or common sense—foolishness. We are appealing to all Christians who have not conceded defeat in the intellectual battle with the world to join us in our efforts to raise a standard to which all men of sound mind can repair.

The love of truth, of God's Word, has all but disappeared in our time. We are committed to and pray for a great instauration. But though we may not see this reformation of Christendom in our lifetimes, we believe it is our duty to present the whole counsel of God because Christ has commanded it. The results of our teaching are in God's hands, not ours. Whatever those results, his Word is never taught in vain, but always accomplishes the result that he intended it to accomplish. Professor Gordon H. Clark has stated our view well:

There have been times in the history of God's people, for example, in the days of Jeremiah, when refreshing grace and widespread revival were not to be expected: the time was one of chastisement. If this twentieth century is of a similar nature, individual Christians here and there can find comfort and strength in a study of God's Word. But if God has decreed happier days for us and if we may expect a world-shaking and genuine spiritual awakening, then it is the author's belief that a zeal for souls, however necessary, is not the sufficient condition. Have there not been devout saints in every age, numerous enough to carry on a revival? Twelve such persons are plenty. What distinguishes the arid ages from the period of the Reformation, when nations were moved as they had not been since Paul preached in Ephesus, Corinth, and Rome, is the latter's fullness of knowledge of God's Word. To echo an early Reformation thought, when the ploughman and the garage attendant know the Bible as well as the theologian does, and know it better than some contemporary theologians, then the desired awakening shall have already occurred.

In addition to publishing books, of which *The Biblical Doctrine of Man* is the seventh, the Foundation publishes a bimonthly newsletter, *The Trinity Review*. Subscriptions to *The Review* are free; please write to the address below to become a subscriber. If you would like further information or would like to join us in our work, please let us know.

The Trinity Foundation is a non-profit foundation tax-exempt under section 501 (c)(3) of the Internal Revenue Code of 1954. You can help us disseminate the Word of God through your tax-deductible contributions to the Foundation.

And we know that the Son of God is come, and hath given us an understanding, that we may know him that is true, and we are in him that is true, in his Son Jesus Christ. This is the true God, and eternal life.

John W. Robbins

Intellectual Ammunition

The Trinity Foundation is committed to the reconstruction of philosophy and theology along Biblical lines. We regard God's command to bring all our thoughts into conformity with Christ very seriously, and the books listed below are designed to accomplish that goal. They are written with two subordinate purposes: (1) to demolish all secular claims to knowledge; and (2) to build a system of truth based upon the Bible alone.

Philosophy

Behaviorism and Christianity, Gordon H. Clark $5.95
       Behaviorism *is a critique of both secular and religious behaviorists. It includes chapters on John Watson, Edgar S. Singer Jr., Gilbert Ryle, B.F. Skinner, and Donald MacKay. Clark's refutation of behaviorism and his argument for a Christian doctrine of man are unanswerable.*

A Christian Philosophy of Education, Gordon H. Clark $8.95
       The first edition of this book was published in 1946. It sparked the contemporary interest in Christian schools. Dr. Clark has thoroughly revised and updated it, and it is needed now more than ever. Its chapters include: The Need for a World-View, The Christian World-View, The

Alternative to Christian Theism, Neutrality, Ethics, The Christian Philoso-phy of Education, Academic Matters, Kindergarten to University. Three appendices are included as well: The Relationship of Public Education to Christianity, A Protestant World-View, and Art and the Gospel.

A Christian View of Men and Things, Gordon H. Clark $10.95

No other book achieves what A Christian View *does: the presenta-tion of Christianity as it applies to history, politics, ethics, science, religion, and epistemology. Clark's command of both worldly philosophy and Scripture is evident on every page, and the result is a breathtaking and invigorating challenge to the wisdom of this world.*

Clark Speaks From The Grave, Gordon H. Clark $3.95

Dr. Clark chides some of his critics for their failure to defend Christianity competently. Clark Speaks *is a stimulating and illuminating discussion of the errors of contemporary apologists.*

Dewey, Gordon H. Clark $2.00

Dewey has had an immense influence on American philosophy and education. His irrationalism, the effects of which we can see in government education, is thoroughly criticized by Clark.

Education, Christianity, and the State $7.95
J. Gresham Machen

Machen was one of the foremost educators, theologians, and defenders of Christianity in the twentieth century. The author of numerous scholarly books, Machen saw clearly that if Christianity is to survive and flourish, a system of Christian grade schools must be established. This collection of essays captures his thought on education over nearly three decades.

Gordon H. Clark: Personal Recollections $6.95
John W. Robbins, editor

Friends of Dr. Clark have written their recollections of the man. Contributors include family members, colleagues, students, and friends such as Harold Lindsell, Carl Henry, Ronald Nash, Dwight Zeller, and

Mary Crumpacker. The book includes an extensive bibliography of Clark's work.

Logic, Gordon H. Clark $8.95
    Written as a textbook for Christian schools, Logic *is another unique book from Clark's pen. His presentation of the laws of thought, which must be followed if Scripture is to be understood correctly, and which are found in Scripture itself, is both clear and thorough.* Logic *is an indispensable book for the thinking Christian.*

The Philosophy of Science and Belief in God $5.95
Gordon H. Clark
    In opposing the contemporary idolatry of science, Clark analyzes three major aspects of science: the problem of motion, Newtonian science, and modern theories of physics. His conclusion is that science, while it may be useful, is always false; and he demonstrates its falsity in numerous ways. Since science is always false, it can offer no objection to the Bible and Christianity.

Religion, Reason and Revelation, Gordon H. Clark $7.95
    One of Clark's apologetical masterpieces, Religion, Reason and Revelation *has been praised for the clarity of its thought and language. It includes chapters on Is Christianity a Religion? Faith and Reason, Inspiration and Language, Revelation and Morality, and God and Evil. It is must reading for all serious Christians.*

Thales to Dewey: A History of Philosophy   paper $11.95
Gordon H. Clark   hardback $16.95
    This volume is the best one volume history of philosophy in English.

Three Types of Religious Philosophy, Gordon H. Clark $6.95
    In this book on apologetics, Clark examines empiricism, rationalism, dogmatism, and contemporary irrationalism, which does not rise to the level of philosophy. He offers a solution to the question, "How can Christianity be defended before the world?"

Theology

The Atonement, Gordon H. Clark $8.95
This is a major addition to Clark's multi-volume systematic theology. In The Atonement, *Clark discusses the Covenants, the Virgin Birth and Incarnation, federal headship and representation, the relationship between God's sovereignty and justice, and much more. He analyzes traditional views of the Atonement and criticizes them in the light of Scripture alone.*

The Biblical Doctrine of Man, Gordon H. Clark $6.95
Is man soul and body or soul, spirit, and body? What is the image of God? Is Adam's sin imputed to his children? Is evolution true? Are men totally depraved? What is the heart? These are some of the questions discussed and answered from Scripture in this book.

Cornelius Van Til: The Man and The Myth $2.45
John W. Robbins
The actual teachings of this eminent Philadelphia theologian have been obscured by the myths that surround him. This book penetrates those myths and criticizes Van Til's surprisingly unorthodox views of God and the Bible.

Faith and Saving Faith, Gordon H. Clark $6.95
The views of the Roman Catholic church, John Calvin, Thomas Manton, John Owen, Charles Hodge, and B.B. Warfield are discussed in this book. Is the object of faith a person or a proposition? Is faith more than belief? Is belief more than thinking with assent, as Augustine said? In a world chaotic with differing views of faith, Clark clearly explains the Biblical view of faith and saving faith.

God's Hammer: The Bible and Its Critics, Gordon H. Clark $6.95
The starting point of Christianity, the doctrine on which all other doctrines depend, is "The Bible alone is the Word of God written, and therefore inerrant in the autographs." Over the centuries the opponents of

Christianity, with Satanic shrewdness, have concentrated their attacks on the truthfulness and completeness of the Bible. In the twentieth century the attack is not so much in the fields of history and archaeology as in philosophy. Clark's brilliant defense of the complete truthfulness of the Bible is captured in this collection of eleven major essays.

Guide to the Westminster Confession and Catechism, $13.95
James E. Bordwine
This large book contains the full text of both the Westminster Confession (both original and American versions) and the Larger Catechism. In addition, it offers a chapter-by-chapter summary of the Confession and a unique index to both the Confession and the Catechism.

The Incarnation, Gordon H. Clark $8.95
Who was Christ? The attack on the Incarnation in the nineteenth and twentieth centuries has been vigorous, but the orthodox response has been lame. Clark reconstructs the doctrine of the Incarnation building upon and improving upon the Chalcedonian definition.

In Defense of Theology, Gordon H. Clark $9.95
There are four groups to whom Clark addresses this book: the average Christians who are uninterested in theology, the atheists and agnostics, the religious experientialists, and the serious Christians. The vindication of the knowledge of God against the objections of three of these groups is the first step in theology.

The Johannine Logos, Gordon H. Clark $5.95
Clark analyzes the relationship between Christ, who is the truth, and the Bible. He explains why John used the same word to refer to both Christ and his teaching. Chapters deal with the Prologue to John's Gospel, Logos and Rheemata, Truth, and Saving Faith.

Logical Criticisms of Textual Criticism, Gordon H. Clark $3.25
In this critique of the science of textual criticism, Dr. Clark exposes the fallacious argumentation of the modern textual critics and defends

*the view that the early Christians knew better than the modern critics
which manuscripts of the New Testament were more accurate.*

Pat Robertson: A Warning to America $6.95
John W. Robbins
   *The Protestant Reformation was based on the Biblical principle that
the Bible is the only revelation from God, yet a growing religious
movement, one of whose spokesmen is Pat Robertson, asserts that God
speaks to them directly. This book addresses the serious issue of religious
fanaticism in America by examining the theological views of televangelist
Pat Robertson.*

Predestination, Gordon H. Clark $8.95
   *Clark thoroughly discusses one of the most controversial and
pervasive doctrines of the Bible: that God is, quite literally, Almighty. Free
will, the origin of evil, God's omniscience, creation, and the new birth are
all presented within a Scriptural framework. The objections of those who
do not believe in the Almighty God are considered and refuted. This
edition also contains the text of the booklet,* Predestination in the Old
Testament.

Scripture Twisting in the Seminaries. Part 1: Feminism $5.95
John W. Robbins
   *An analysis of the views of three graduates of Westminster Seminary
on the role of women in the church.*

Today's Evangelism: Counterfeit or Genuine? $6.95
Gordon H. Clark
   *Clark compares the methods and messages of today's evangelists
with Scripture, and finds that Christianity is on the wane because the
Gospel has been distorted or lost. This is an extremely useful and
enlightening book.*

The Trinity, Gordon H. Clark $8.95
   *Apart from the doctrine of Scripture, no teaching of the Bible is
more important than the doctrine of God. Clark's defense of the*

orthodox doctrine of the Trinity is a principal portion of a major new work of Systematic Theology now in progress. There are chapters on the deity of Christ, Augustine, the incomprehensibility of God, Bavinck and Van Til, and the Holy Spirit, among others.

What Do Presbyterians Believe? Gordon H. Clark $7.95
   This classic introduction to Christian doctrine has been republished. It is the best commentary on the Westminster Confession of Faith ever written.

Commentaries on the New Testament

Colossians, Gordon H. Clark $6.95
Ephesians, Gordon H. Clark $8.95
First Corinthians, Gordon H. Clark $10.95
First and Second Thessalonians, Gordon H. Clark $5.95
The Pastoral Epistles (I and II Timothy and Titus) $9.95
   Gordon H. Clark

   All of Clark's commentaries are expository, not technical, and are written for the Christian layman. His purpose is to explain the text clearly and accurately so that the Word of God will be thoroughly understood by every Christian.

The Trinity Library

We will send you one copy of each of the 33 books listed above for the low price of $150. The regular price of these books is $240. You may also order the books you want individually on the order blank on the next page. Because some of the books are in short supply, we must reserve the right to substitute others of equal or greater value in The Trinity Library.

Thank you for your attention. We hope to hear from you soon. This special offer expires June 30, 1994.

Order Form

Name _____

Address _____

_____

Please: □ add my name to the mailing list for *The Trinity Review*. I understand that there is no charge for the *Review*.

□ accept my tax deductible contribution of $ _____ for the work of the Foundation.

□ send me _____ copies of *The Biblical Doctrine of Man*. I enclose as payment $ _____.

□ send me the Trinity Library of 33 books. I enclose $150 as full payment for it.

□ send me the following books. I enclose full payment in the amount of $ _____ for them.

_____

_____

_____

_____

_____

_____

Mail to: The Trinity Foundation
                Post Office Box 700
                Jefferson, MD 21755

Please add $2.00 for postage on orders less than $10. Thank you.
For quantity discounts, please write to the Foundation.